Championing Women Leaders

Championing Women Leaders

Beyond Sponsorship

Shaheena Janjuha-Jivraj

Director, Boardwalk Leadership, UK

Kitty Chisholm

Director, Boardwalk Leadership, UK

First published 2016 by
PALGRAVE MACMILLAN

Palgrave Macmillan in the UK is an imprint of Macmillan Publishers Limited, registered in England, company number 785998, of Houndmills, Basingstoke, Hampshire RG21 6XS.

Palgrave Macmillan in the US is a division of St Martin's Press LLC, 175 Fifth Avenue, New York, NY 10010.

Palgrave Macmillan is the global academic imprint of the above companies and has companies and representatives throughout the world.

Palgrave® and Macmillan® are registered trademarks in the United States, the United Kingdom, Europe and other countries.

ISBN 978–1–137–47893–1   hardback

This book is printed on paper suitable for recycling and made from fully managed and sustained forest sources. Logging, pulping and manufacturing processes are expected to conform to the environmental regulations of the country of origin.

A catalogue record for this book is available from the British Library.

A catalog record for this book is available from the Library of Congress.

Typeset by MPS Limited, Chennai, India.

Shaheena
For Surinder and Amina and Sohail for their constant support.
For my husband Zahir – thank you for everything. For my boys,
Iliyan, Kais, and Zayn, for the champions they will become.

Kitty
For Aleca and Greg, Alexander, Katarina, Jovan, Toma, and
Zanthe, Alexandra, Roderick, and my husband John,
without whose proactive support and encouragement
this book would not have been possible.

Contents

List of Figures and Tables

Figures

Tables

Preface

"We are not measured by the number of champions we create, but by the number of opportunities we create for others to be champions in life." *Billie Jean King*

Billie Jean King's speech to the United Nations Office on Sport for Development and Peace in April 2015 was about creating more opportunities for sports women and men. To us, this quote says everything about championing women into every aspect of leadership. This book is about championing women leaders. Why championing? Because as a champion you have succeeded, you have competed under the toughest conditions, and thrown every resource you have into winning. Championing is about winning! It's about getting results. We are very clear: championing is results-focused; it's about investing in human talent to get the best results for any organization.

We define championing of women as **proactive support and advocacy that advances a woman's leadership aspirations with care for her well-being as a person**. The core of championing lies in the relationship between the champion, a senior leader who has the ability to influence their peers who are decision-makers, and the "one to watch" (OTW)[1] an individual rising through an organization with talent and aspirations requiring guidance in navigating promotional routes, support, and an advocate. The championing relationship bundles a number of support

---

[1] For ease we have abbreviated "one to watch" to OTW throughout the book.

mechanisms into a relationship. Inevitably, one champion cannot perform all of these roles and the OTW may have multiple champions or different champions at different times in their career paths. What championing offers, unlike mentoring or even sponsorship, is the ability to combine support for the individual, career development, and a means of navigating the organization through a relationship based on trust and longer-term investment in human potential.

With this premise we see championing as a win–win for everyone: for the OTW, who is able to achieve acceleration in their careers; for the champion, who as a leader aspires to build strong succession; and for the organization, to ensure it consistently has access to more than 50 per cent of the talent pool.

Why then focus on women? Although a great deal of progress is being made by women in all areas of leadership, the rate of change is not fast enough. The UN states: "Today no country has achieved gender equality across all areas of public and private life and significant inequalities persist between women and men."[2] Championing women provides an opportunity to address these inequalities, to advocate and promote human talent, and enable women to achieve their leadership potential.

We have focused on championing at work, in the context of women's careers and businesses because we know the challenges that women face during this phase of life contribute to the dearth of women leaders. Of course, the principles of championing can be applied at any point from early childhood, schooling, through university, and beyond. What makes championing so compelling is the opportunities it provides to women at any stage in their career; if they have leadership aspirations and credibility, champions can be a powerful force in their promotion.

Championing is about organizations accessing the best possible resources they need to remain competitive. In the "war for talent,"[3] senior leaders

---

[2] www.unwomen.org/media/headquarters/attachments/sections/news/stories/2015/stepitup-calltoaction-chile-en.pdf.
[3] A term first used by Steven Hankin of McKinsey & Company in 1997.

need to have well-honed skills in spotting and developing human potential for their organizations to perform. There is growing evidence demonstrating that companies with a strong mix of men and women at board and senior executive levels perform better than those without. Our argument is simple; having a critical mass of women at senior levels in organizations improves performance, increasing innovation and raising the quality of decision-making.

Acknowledgments

A book of this scope is only achievable by virtue of the immense support we have received from family, friends, and colleagues. There are a few people we want to thank specially for their wonderful support and specific help: our colleague Diana Theodores, who has provided the most inspirational creativity to our thinking; our research and writing team, Darta Jace, Jeremy Hazlehurst, Ashiana Jivraj, and Farzana Velji; colleagues at the Commonwealth Secretariat and Commonwealth Business Women communities; ministers and advisors who shared their views and opinions anonymously. So many people have been generous in reaching out with sparkling enthusiasm and facilitating introductions to the women and men we interviewed: Sandra Alevra, Diana Carney, Judy Foster, Amanda Holmes, Shachi Irde, Alex Johnston, Yasmin Lakhani, Catherine Mulder, Sonal Thrakar, Daiga Trumpe.

Naaz Coker passed away in September 2015. Her vision and spirit will continue to be shared in the stories of her leadership and we are grateful to have had the opportunity to include her voice in our book.

Our most profound thanks to all those we interviewed, formally and informally, named and anonymous, to the women and men who shared their stories with us, who inspired us with their wisdom, their courage, their generosity, and their commitment to championing talent wherever they could find it. Thanks also to all the participants on our leadership development programmes, for your challenges, your commitment to change, and your remarkable achievements.

And finally, our gratitude to our editorial team at Palgrave, especially Josie Taylor, Francesca White, Stephen Partridge, and Julie Rowbotham.

Introduction

Where it all began

Shaheena and Kitty have worked in business, academia, and the public sector, combining 65 years of experience across 65 countries. Our relationship began as one of champion and "one to watch" (OTW), with Kitty as Director of Development, who spotted potential in Shaheena, who had just returned to work after her first maternity leave. Shaheena could see the opportunity in developing a relationship with Kitty, who was at that time developing new income channels. Kitty saw in Shaheena someone with entrepreneurial flair, an authoritative presence, and a great deal of untapped potential.

Our championing relationship evolved considerably over time. We had experience of working with women across different sectors and in different types of organizations, shared similar values and could see the urgent need for more women in leadership – not just in the UK, but in every country we had worked in. We were also passionate about creating new, genuinely effective ways of training, educating, and developing human talent. This is how we joined forces and with our third partner, Diana Theodores, created Boardwalk Leadership, a company dedicated to supporting women in realizing their leadership potential.

Building the evidence

Our work had introduced us, with admiration and delight, to talented, motivated, hard-working women in hundreds of very different kinds of organizations, across six continents: large companies (private and public), entrepreneurial start-ups, family businesses, social enterprises, public sector organizations, theatres, schools, universities, charities, pretty much every type of organization possible. We knew from the literature, and from our own time teaching in different universities, that women were now outperforming men at university. We also knew that many organizations were recruiting equal numbers of women and men. What we couldn't understand was why equal numbers of women were not reaching the most senior levels of organizations, regardless of the sector. Our initial research identified a number of reasons – in which the women were at the heart of the issue: they weren't ambitious enough, they preferred to opt out of the workplace to spend more time with their family, they weren't committed to the hours needed for the top jobs, and there weren't enough appropriately experienced or qualified women! Despite the findings, we saw it very differently and we started to dig deeper. We were very grateful to Sylvia Ann Hewlett of the Center for Talent Innovation (CTI) for her insightful work on sponsorship,[1] which moved the discussion along enormously.

Our own working experiences and the hundreds of women we had met as a result, the careers of our friends, colleagues, and relatives challenged the prevailing discourse. We felt there was a significant dichotomy between what was being said about women and what women were really saying about themselves and their leadership journeys. So we launched a major piece of research in conjunction with Liz St Clair of Women in Public Policy (WIPP) at the House of Lords in the UK in 2011, asking women what was stopping them from accessing leadership roles. At this time, most of these discussions in the UK were dominated by the FTSE 100 companies and we wanted to know what was going on beyond this group, where the majority of women worked. We targeted women across all sectors and industries. They came from a broad cross-section of organizations; multinationals, entrepreneurial businesses, privately-owned family businesses, government departments, charities, social enterprises. Our fundamental question was – what is getting in the way of their leadership aspirations?

The results were staggering, by virtue of the consistency of responses we received. We were blown away by the clustering of responses around five themes, despite the immense diversity of respondents. It did not seem to matter what type, size, or sector of organization these women worked in, they were telling us that the same things were in their way. Our results showed a complex environment for women in leadership, in which most of what was getting in their way was cultural and organizational, rather than about their own choices, experiences, ambitions, or qualifications. But in order to understand how to address the barriers, we felt we needed to know more about what was happening in and across industries and even countries.

Here was part of the problem; there was not enough reliable data beyond the US and Western Europe to identify the number of women in leadership roles. Organizations such as Catalyst in Canada had been doing a brilliant job in sourcing data, but there was still not enough to understand what was really affecting the position of women in leadership in different sectors. This line of investigation led us to co-author a report with Arif Zaman from the Commonwealth Business Council, benchmarking the number of women in business leadership roles in the Commonwealth countries. Again, we were in for a shock; only 18 out of 53 countries collected data on women in business leadership positions. Without the facts, companies, sectors, and even countries could not be held accountable for what they did or did not do to support women into leadership. And without this it was clear the problem would still remain for the women. The report was presented at the Commonwealth Heads of Government Meeting in Sri Lanka in 2013 and the recommendations we suggested were accepted – every single one. Our recommendations included:

- The creation of a database of board-ready (and board-potential) women.
- Supporting sponsoring initiatives.

- Building a research monitor across the Commonwealth.
- Raising career aspirations.
- Creating a media strategy that clearly and objectively demonstrates the impact of women in senior leadership positions, to enable stakeholders to make informed choices; this includes customers and investors.
- Sharing best practice across the Commonwealth.

Our research demonstrated that more needed to be done for women, especially within organizations. Between 2014 and 2015, we conducted a follow-up piece of work to examine women's progress into leadership across the Commonwealth. With the diversity of countries in the Commonwealth, we expected to identify widely different patterns impacting women into leadership.

Our expectations were again confounded. We were taken aback by how similar their experiences were, not only across organizations but also across cultures and levels of economic development. This time we focused not only on their perceptions of the barriers but also on what had helped them to achieve their success.

Listening to the women we interviewed was truly inspiring; every story shared built up a kaleidoscope of experiences. These were women who came from such a wide range of backgrounds, they did not all fit the mold of privilege with financially comfortable families and Ivy League education. A few did, but many more were characterized by challenging childhoods and backgrounds, migration at a young age, unconventional routes into the work place, and barriers from teachers, lecturers, colleagues, and line managers. Each of these women is a leader: from ministers of state to entrepreneurial company founders; chief executives of listed companies to artistic directors; senior partners in law firms to heads of charities; bankers to professors and vice-chancellors; board directors of family firms to senior engineers in global aerospace or construction businesses.

So we felt we should try to capture the privilege we had experienced in listening to these women and we wanted to make our learning available to others. Almost every woman we spoke to recognized how they had been championed and helped us to shape our thinking. In this book, we use their stories to illustrate what really works for individuals and organizations. We share the stories to demonstrate how these women raise the visibility of championship, and what power and value can be unleashed when women with great potential, the OTWs, are truly championed in every sense of the word.

Leadership and Championship

We do not assume that all women, or indeed all men, want to be leaders. We don't all want the same things at the same times, and indeed our aspirations and aims change throughout our lives. As Geraldine Haley, Global Head of Executive Talent and Succession, Standard Chartered, said at a gathering of Inspirational Women at Gallup, London, in early 2015, "Remember, you are not now the person you will be in ten years' time." We would go even further, you are not now the person you will be in one year's time, and indeed, your brain will have changed by the time you finish reading this paragraph!

We do not define leadership only in terms of the C-Suite of FTSE100,[2] or S&P 500,[3] but include leadership of teams at various levels in organizations, as reflected in all the work and research we carry out. We also recognize that leadership takes different forms at many levels. It is contextual and situational, and so much more than positional. You may not think of yourself as a leader, but there may be times when you act like one, when you *are* one for others because you can see clearly what needs to be done when they cannot, even if you do not have leader, director, or manager anywhere near your title or role. If you have people who follow you willingly, who really hear what you say and understand what you do and are influenced by that, who willingly want to support you in achieving certain goals, you are a leader. As Claire Felice Pace, from the Ministry of Education in Malta, states: "Leaders need to leave something sustainable – empower others so that they share your vision."

When we were involved in the creation of a leadership academy for a security services company based in the UK, we noticed that many talented women and men in the middle of the organization did not see themselves as leaders. These were individuals who had risen from the ranks and were running key frontline divisions, sometimes with more than 300 people reporting to them. We were able to help them think differently about their role and what they did on a daily basis. We enabled them to viscerally understand how what they did, and how they did it, impacted on the people they led, how they could release and nurture talent and innovation or stifle it, how they could create environments that motivated themselves and others.

We have seen that ways in which people demonstrate leadership are increasingly diverse, and this makes leadership far more fluid. The impact of increasingly global economies: borders redrawn, disruptive technologies creating new business and political models, also creates different interpretations of leadership. We have seen time and time again that the quality of leadership across the organization, as well as top down, can make the biggest difference to execution. We see it as crucial that we support women in enabling them to make genuine choices for their own brand of leadership. Essentially, our job is to help women become leaders IF THAT IS WHAT THEY REALLY WANT. We need to make sure women don't step away from the leadership table because they don't believe they can get to it.

Some people see the cost of leadership – the demands of time and energy – being just too much. Others have other priorities at certain times in their lives, such as taking on a charitable role, trekking across South America, writing a book, or raising children. Some people are very happy running parts of organizations, or being a brilliant number two, a COO focusing on delivering day in day out rather than a CEO who has to satisfy all stakeholders, grow the share price and market share in the face of global turbulence. The immense change in lifestyle and working patterns means that the attraction of "having it all" is no longer the only mantra for both women and men.

Your ambitions will drive what you want and ultimately your influence and impact. You can aim for what you want if you know what that is.

Remember that ambitions change and can grow. You can be a successful and content number two, leading your own teams. And sometimes you wake up one morning and realize that you could do your boss' job better and that you are now ready and eager to take on the top job; that what looked like a sacrifice before now looks trivial compared to the enjoyment and creative freedom you will exercise, growing yourself and others, at the very top of your organization – be it a government department, multinational organization, or your family's enterprise. And sometimes you don't, and you realize that the difference you want to make in the world as a result of being in it is in a different mold. We agree with Sheryl Sandberg's view on leadership: "We can each define ambition and progress for ourselves. The goal is to work toward a world where expectations are not set by the stereotypes that hold us back, but by our personal passion, talents and interests."[4]

So if you think that you want to be a successful leader, at whatever level, whether right now or in the future, this book is for you. If you want to change your organization so as to make it more diverse, a better environment for both women and men to fulfill their potential and perform consistently at their best, then this book is for you, too!

How we work

This book is a reflection of our approach as facilitators, coaches, and teachers. We engage the mind and body, the emotions and "rational" brain in all aspects of our work. We have applied this practice to the two dimensions of the printed page through our thinking, the case studies, and tasks. Our approach is evidence-based and we have pulled together the latest thinking from a range of research, along with our own empirical research. We have looked at what happens at governmental, organizational, and individual levels to propel more women into leadership. And we have listened to the stories of women from across the world.

In the same way as we deliver awareness, training, and development programs, we do not offer a single solution to what we acknowledge is a multifaceted problem. We offer a range of options, activities, and ideas for you to try out for yourselves, with colleagues, within your teams, with friends and family. Some of the tasks will help you to examine what is going on in your organization and how you can create change.

We provide you with the evidence we have collected in our research of women's experiences along their various paths to leadership in the 21st century, having also spoken to champions, advocates who repeatedly emphasized the need to invest in and develop talent. We distill the evidence into discussion of what it means, into a range of suggestions and recommended tasks to help you find the actions that best suit you and your circumstances.

How to use this book

This book draws upon the findings of our research in the UK, Europe, the Americas, and across the Commonwealth, to provide an evidence-based foundation for the discussion of what more can be done to enable even more women into senior leadership roles. Each chapter presents another layer for the championing relationships, from the CHAMP model in the first chapter to understanding how championing works in practice and what you need to do to maintain the relationship. Each chapter presents a discussion based on our review of current thinking and research, along with relevant case studies that highlight the behavioral and attitudinal components. The end of each chapter has a selection of tasks, along with suggestions for further reading and additional resources.

Stories are a powerful aspect of any leadership journey. They can draw you in and help you understand the perspective of the storyteller. We know stories not only stir emotions but also create powerful lessons and examples and allow us to make sense of experiences. We place a great deal of emphasis on how leadership stories emerge, are crafted, refined, and shaped. We have shared with you the inspiring connections we experienced on listening to stories of the women we spoke to, and have worked to craft those stories to share with you. We have introduced our own story, the story of Maya,[5] an educated, accomplished woman with the world seemingly at her feet, who has experiences many readers will relate to. We explore how her life evolves and her career aspirations take flight and, when she stalls, we examine how she gains momentum and re-establishes some of her lost passion and focus, how she re-launches her career.

chapter 1

The CHAMP Model

Our story starts with a young girl, Maya, an enthusiastic youngster with parents who gave her a wide range of experiences and encouraged her to go for challenging goals. As she progressed through school she excelled in her studies and consistently achieved strong grades. She was a model pupil, straight "A" student, a great team player, a member of the student council. As Maya completed her schooling she successfully applied to study at a leading university. During her degree program she continued to go from strength to strength, her grades continued to remain strong and she managed to secure an internship opportunity in a world-class company. Upon graduation she had the pick of job offers. Interested in traveling and experiencing other cultures, she chose an international telecoms company that happened to have an equal split of males and females at graduate entry level.

Women in leadership – where are we now?

Women have achieved significant progress in leadership in a relatively short space of time. If we look at the Fortune 500 companies, 25 of the CEOs are women, and 20 years ago the list did not contain any women.[1] But in reality these women only constitute 5 per cent of the CEO roles on the Fortune list. The progress is there but we haven't achieved enough and we are not moving quickly enough. Despite the immense progress in new business models and substantial shifts in global boundaries, the situation of women in leadership seems to have become stuck. In 2011, when Shaheena was involved in the EU debate on quotas, Norway was constantly flagged up as a shining example of what could be done to create more opportunities for getting women into leadership positions. Four years on, the examples of good practice and progress have not changed very much, even though we are now looking at a broader global platform. Based on progress to date, the UN estimates we will achieve gender parity in the workplace in 2096, and remuneration for work of equal value in 2090. What this really means is that neither our daughters, nor their daughters will achieve true parity, but if we are lucky it will happen with our great-granddaughters. Furthermore, women will achieve parity in decision-making in 2045. These statistics make for sobering thoughts about how much progress we have really made.

Despite the presence of women in education, not enough is being done to harness the power of this group into the economy. It is astonishing that the talents of over 50 per cent of human beings are not being fully harnessed to decision-making at the most senior levels in politics, public service, business, and civil society. Christine Lagarde, the first female Managing Director of the International Monetary Fund, has argued that gender equality is a necessary economic principle and is not simply about social justice. She is clear about the need to involve both women and men in order to achieve global economic recovery, as stated in her keynote speech, "The Economic Power of Women's Empowerment," given in Tokyo in September 2014:[2]

> Today more than ever, the global economy needs precisely this kind of radiant sun – to provide light and nourishment. To provide healing. To dry out the swamps of poverty and unrest. The reason is obvious. Seven years into the worst global financial crisis since the Great Depression, the recovery is still too tepid and too turbulent. And even after the crisis abates, we will face grave challenges to growth – as a slower "new normal" sets in, as populations age, and as economic disparities

increase. Given these challenges, we will need all the economic growth, dynamism and ingenuity we can get in the years ahead. Thankfully, a key part of the solution is staring us right in the face – unleashing the economic power of women. Bringing the world's largest excluded group into the fold.

Identifying support structures for the "world's largest excluded group" is complex, particularly in a relatively fragmented environment. Whilst a great deal of excellent work has focused on women in North America and Western Europe, we wanted to take a global perspective to identify the challenges women faced in their leadership goals. As we work in a globally mobile environment, we felt it important to identify and develop support structures for women that are seamless and so allow women to benefit wherever they are based.

The debate on women in leadership is firmly split into two halves and often resembles a tennis match, with both sides furiously lobbing demands at each other to either "fix" the women or to "fix" the organizations. We find this kind of language singularly unhelpful. We believe that the responsibility for accelerating the pace for gender equality in leadership is shared – between individuals – men and women – organizations and states.

Championing crystallizes a number of the areas that need to be addressed in order to make progress for women in leadership. We would argue that championing provides the essential relationship needed to create opportunities for talent promotion. However, to understand the immense potential of championing, it needs to be understood within its framework – what we have devised to illustrate and apply this is the CHAMP model.

The CHAMP model presents drivers for championing (see Figure 1.1). It provides a framework for action for women aspiring to leadership roles and for everyone in organizations committed to ensuring that the best of human talent has every possible opportunity to achieve leadership aspirations.

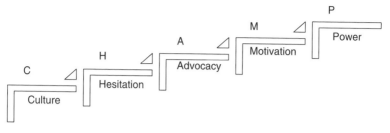

FIGURE 1.1 The CHAMP model

Source: ©Shaheena Janjuha-Jivraj, 2015.

C is for Culture

The environment plays a significant role in leadership and economic opportunities for women. Country legislation around gender equality in the workplace, which varies across regions, creates environments that will encourage or inhibit female economic participation and leadership opportunities. In Chapter 2, we will explore this in more detail by measuring the relationship between the country rankings on the annual Global Gender Gap report produced by the World Economic Forum and our data on the number of female executive and non-executive directors in privately listed companies.

Industry sectors also create significant influence on attitudes towards women in the workplace, particularly in circumstances where they have traditionally been male-dominated. The culture of sectors should not be underestimated, even in countries with well-established gender equality legislation in place. Policies may be in place but attitudes take a lot longer to change. Consider, for example, the case of Canada, a country with a strong emphasis on education, a good track record of gender equality legislation in the workplace, and a very diverse population. One of its provinces, Quebec, has quotas in place for women on boards in SOEs (state-owned enterprises).[3] Despite having all of these structures in place, only

12 per cent of board positions are held by women.[4] Canada's economy is dominated by sectors that have a long-standing history of male dominance, including Energy (oil and gas), Agriculture, and Manufacturing.[5]

Countries that have the right legal frameworks to support gender equality do minimize the impact of discrimination and provide legal requirements for compulsory education of both genders until the completion of secondary schooling. Interestingly, these conditions do not automatically create parity in gender leadership. They certainly help to level out the playing field and create opportunities to achieve a baseline of gender equality in terms of university education and ability to learn and develop the right technical and specialist skills for certain sectors such as Medicine, Maths, Engineering, and Law. We are all more or less familiar with the stats on female graduates who occupy around 50 per cent of graduate jobs, and how these numbers drastically tail off by the time they reach middle-management level.

The different terminology applied to this phenomenon, whether the glass cliff or waterfall,[6] identifies and reinforces the significant dropout rate of women 10–15 years into their careers. The attrition rate has a staggering impact on business performance; Cascio (2006) estimated a direct replacement was likely to cost 150–200 per cent of the salary of a skilled individual.[7] If we measure the cost of churn as the number of people lost, multiplied by the costs of direct replacement, the numbers really ramp up when we consider the loss of women along the pipeline.

Figure 1.2 shows the attrition rate of women from graduate entry to C-Suite level.

The figures are likely to be even higher when we include the indirect costs associated with staff turnover, which may involve accrued paid time off and the costs associated with finding a replacement – not to mention loss of productivity during the transition period. In Chapter 5, we will discuss the reasons and challenges faced by organizations and how to engender a strong and transparent championing culture.

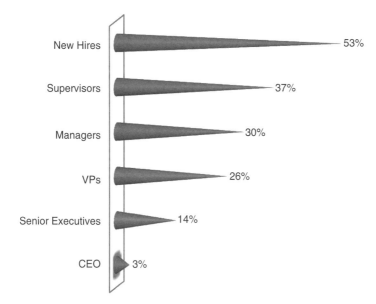

New Hires — 53%

Supervisors — 37%

Managers — 30%

VPs — 26%

Senior Executives — 14%

CEO — 3%

FIGURE 1.2 / Attrition rate of women from graduate entry to C-Suite level

Source: ©Zenger Folkman 2009.[8]

H is for Hesitation

When constructing the CHAMP model, we questioned the inclusion of hesitation, primarily because of its negative connotations. Having considered the obvious implications, we knew that to remove it would be to ignore the very root of what really holds women back. We know that despite cultural differences, on the whole there are similar reasons why women hold back and the impact it has on leadership opportunities. In Chapter 3, we discuss the behaviors and implications of women hesitating to step into leadership spaces and identify some really powerful ways forward.

Hesitancy to step up for roles is due to a combination of things. The much-cited Hewlett Packard internal report states that men will apply for a job if they tick 60 per cent of the criteria (experience and qualifications), whereas women will only apply if they align with 100 per cent of the characteristics. Work by Tara Mohr in 2014 followed up on these statistics by surveying over a thousand American professionals, both men and women, to determine whether there were gender differences in attitudes towards applying for jobs when they did not meet all the qualifications.[9] Her research showed 15 per cent of the women stated they were following guidelines, in contrast to 8 per cent of the male respondents. In addition, just over a fifth of the women (22 per cent) stated they did not want to put themselves out there if they were likely to fail.

We can see why hesitancy is a big piece in leadership and why women need more transparency to understand how the game is being played. We share these examples later on in the book. Sheryl Sandberg's call for women to "Lean In" is a direct response to their hesitation in the workplace, which has most certainly resulted in an avalanche of activity.[10]

Champions need to be adept at recognizing hesitation and handling it, particularly when women are feeling stretched or are at vulnerable points in their careers – for example, a move to a new region, returning after maternity leave, changing roles, or changing teams. Throughout this book, we discuss a variety of reasons why extremely talented and capable women say no to opportunities. In our discussions we have some fantastic examples where women initially said no and their champions convinced them, in a supportive manner, to say yes.

There is another form of hesitancy we want to call out at this stage and this is amongst champions themselves. Taking on a championing role is a strong commitment to promoting human talent and leveling out the playing field. Championing is far more effective when it is transparent and the norm within an organization. If it remains secretive it falls prey to the same allegations around favoritism in the old boys' network and becomes yet another wasted resource. So let's be clear: champions need to be vocal and step up and get credit for investing their time and effort. Furthermore, by creating much more awareness around championing we are likely to develop the traits and behaviors that are crucial for talent development, to ensure that the women who benefit from championing today pay it forward to female talent coming through the pipeline.

A is for Advocacy

Championship relies on action and change through advocacy. For advocacy to be really effective, the advocate needs to believe in a purpose and commit to changing the status quo. Champions for human talent are individuals who first and foremost believe in a level playing field to ensure talent has equal opportunity to rise to the top. Steven Cooper, Head of Personal Banking at Barclays Bank, talks about the changes introduced in Barclays to create a more balanced playing field for female talent; the focus for Barclays has been to address how the company attracts 100 per cent of the talent, not just 50 per cent. The business case is becoming increasingly clear, overlooking female talent means a company is ignoring 80 per cent of the purchasing power in the world.[11]

Advocacy requires champions to create opportunities for female talent and these opportunities will vary enormously. At its most basic level, advocacy raises the profile of female talent to groups of key decision-makers, to which the champion may belong. For example, champions may provide opportunities for stretch roles within the same company and this may involve a step towards promotion. Or it may be recommending female talent for roles and opportunities that allow their talent to shine. Advocacy, as distinct from mentoring and sponsorship, is a much longer-term relationship; the championing relationships that we have seen to be really effective traverse organizational boundaries. Championing works at its most effective when the values of the champion and the "one to watch" (OTW) are aligned and we discuss this further in Chapter 4. Sonal Thakrar in the UK describes the impact of championing from her perspective as an OTW: "I have had so many people backing me – you need the support around you, you need people around you. One of the people I spoke to said, 'I champion you ... I talk about you to senior leaders.'"

We share cases where champions demonstrate a longer-term relationship, having spotted talent the relationship grows and the OTW steps up into the opportunities enabled by the champion. Through the process of pure talent development, the champion continues to build the relationship, creating further progression opportunities for the OTW.

This relationship demonstrates a really tangible example of how leadership branding works.

In Chapter 6, we discuss the importance of building and raising the visibility of a leadership brand. Branding and championing naturally work in synch with each other. The pressure for companies to address talent is increasing and as Victor Oladapo observes, "Companies will have to actively wage war for talent in order to get the right people with the right skills into their organizations."[12]

The World Economic Forum argues that companies have to adjust their competitive basis from tangible assets to intellectual property and services, creating the shift from "capitalism to talentism."[13] Senior leaders need to demonstrate a strong track record in talent management as part of their broader leadership brand. Championing provides a means to develop this skill and demonstrate success by allowing champions to align their leadership brand with upcoming talent. To realize the potential of brand alignment, let's take a step back to 1954. Audrey Hepburn received an Oscar for Best Actress for *Roman Holiday*, wearing a dress by a relatively unknown designer, Hubert de Givenchy. He became an instant sensation and their lengthy collaboration created some of the most iconic fashion designs that still enthral us today.

M is for Motivation

When we refer to motivation in the CHAMP model, we are talking about the desire to invest in and develop human talent, to ensure the best talent has an equal opportunity to rise to the surface. The organization needs to have a strong desire to achieve this and to understand fully what will motivate its leaders and managers to change their behaviors. Organizations that are absolutely committed to tapping into their widest talent pool understand the costs associated with changing structures, developing policies, and creating ways to ensure change is achieved and maintained. It requires an investment of human and even financial capital. When companies ask us about the return on investment for focusing on women's leadership (and yes, they still ask that question) we have the evidence; improved financial performance of companies with diverse boards, high costs of attrition, the growth of the female market. When we talk to companies, we are very clear that this is about business first and foremost and so the investment in the talent pool of a company is as essential as investing in a good marketing strategy.

We know this process is hard work, primarily because of the individual and cultural complexities, and so to overcome the barriers that arise time and again it is crucial to have a clear understanding of what the motivations are. This is equally important within the championing relationship. Champions have a clear sense of their motivation and we have seen this amongst every champion we have spoken to – they are committed to nurturing talent. The champions in our research share their desires to support talent, to make it easier for the next group of talented women to come through, and to ensure their organization has the best group of people, both men and women, leading the company. We have discussed earlier in this chapter why talent development is sought after as a key leadership competency and we will continue this strand of the discussion throughout.

For a champion to invest their resources – by which we mean, time, effort, knowledge, networks, and frankly an element of risk – they need to really understand what motivates their OTW. This is the core that drives behavior and decisions. What are their values and how do they impact the style of the nascent leader? Creating a strong sense of self-awareness around what impacts your decisions provides a very clear connection to creating a strong and authentic style of leadership.

A large number of our women leaders described their commitment to social or voluntary causes and these were as important as their professional careers. Inevitably for many of these leaders the two became intertwined. Through this we have clear evidence that the social- and values-based behaviors are not submerged and pulled out during training sessions but are articulated on a daily basis in leadership practice.

P is for Power

Leadership is about having the power both to make the changes you envisage and to take responsibility for your decisions. The impact of women in political leadership has been recognized over a longer period, with many countries promoting greater female participation through quotas, and ensuring female politicians have access to positions that will make an impact on promoting greater gender equality for women. The figures on the economics of women are also increasing and the focus on women in corporate leadership is about the untapped potential that they bring to global economic recovery. In 2009, Michael Silverstein and Kate Sayre estimated the female market to be worth $20 trillion rising to $28 trillion by 2014, representing a growth market more than twice as big as China and India combined.[14]

Marketers have long recognized the impact of female decision-making. Asia is currently witnessing the immense rise of female consumerism as women make the decision on purchases for 94 per cent of home furnishings, 92 per cent of vacations, 91 per cent of homes, 60 per cent of automobiles, and 51 per cent of consumer electronics. The figures are staggering and likely to continue to rise. In China, growth in the female high-end luxury market is outstripping the male market, and women are fueling the growth of online shopping with 69 per cent of respondents in a survey stating a preference for online shopping.[15] With these facts, we are clear about the growth of the female market and its impact on economic opportunities. Until companies have the right intelligence fed into their decision-making across all levels of their organizations, the potential of this market growth will not be realized. In Christine Lagarde's speech, at the beginning of this chapter, she referred to women as the largest excluded group providing a significant part of the solution to economic recovery by "unleashing the ***economic power of women***." Moving forward is only part of the problem, the pace of change is also critical, as described by Dame Jenny Shipley, former Prime Minister of New Zealand: "Some companies realize it's just good for business and are making real efforts to appoint women, for others it's just not on their agenda. Overall it's positive rather than neutral or negative, but speed is still a frustration for me."

Through this discussion we can see how the CHAMP model provides a framework for championing, supporting women through the pipeline step by step. This model becomes a powerful tool, providing a framework for organizations and individuals, champions and the OTWs to stop the leaky pipeline, and in so doing allow more women to reach the top and create a more powerful and diverse leadership team that can really add value to business and society – a view that has traction with influencers in this field. Helena Morrissey, founder of the 30% Club, states her role has been to create a catalyst "to build relationships with Chairmen who had the influence to champion women and initiate changes to the composition of boards and at all organizational levels," with the emphasis on "a group of business leaders determined to see change."

Tasks

1. A bit of blue-sky thinking for your ambitions.

In order to successfully develop a championing relationship you need to know what your ambitions are. As an OTW, you have potential, but where are you directing your energy/career? At this stage if you don't have goals, that's OK, but you certainly have ambition, otherwise you wouldn't be reading this book. What does that ambition look like? If you were creating a picture that would sum up your achievements in 10, 20, or 30 years' time, what would it look like? What would be different in the future? There are various ways you can do this and an easy one would be to create a mood board; either virtually or with good old-fashioned magazines and photos. A mood board, often used by designers, is a powerful visual tool to help create a sense of a new collection before the pieces are fully formed.

Take some time to think about what your success would look like; you may not be able to define it too clearly but the images will allow you to generate a sense of how it would feel and what it might resemble. For now, that's more than enough.

When you have finished assembling your mood board, take some photographs of it, keep them accessible, either on your phone, laptop, or tablet, and if you can print out a couple of images and stick them in a place where you can see them regularly, they will become a powerful visual aid for a time when you are setting clearer goals.

2. Consider the following questions and note down your answers either in a journal or on your laptop. Where possible try to keep all your notes and reflections together so they form part of your bigger plan moving forward.

C is for Culture	How does your organization encourage and enable diversity?
H is for Hesitation	Identify three areas where you are most likely to hesitate: Consider – Why? What stops you?
A is for Advocacy	Who in your organization is a natural advocate? How do you align yourself to them - what does your big picture look like? Don't spend too much time on this – note down initial thoughts. Write down in one sentence what you hope to achieve through your career.
M is for Motivation	What really motivates you? What is it you enjoy the most? What gets you out of bed on a miserable grey day?
P is for Power	When have you been at your most powerful? What did it look like? How did you feel? What was the impact of your power?

For organizations:

C is for Culture	How does the organization encourage and enable diversity? What have you done specifically to promote greater gender diversity in your organization?
H is for Hesitation	Within your organization, what are the areas where you are most likely to lose women? How is this information used to inform diversity and inclusion policies?
A is for Advocacy	How much attention does your organization give to understanding the ambitions of staff during annual appraisals? How are senior executives encouraged to advocate upcoming talent?
M is for Motivation	How does your organization encourage staff to perform at their best?
P is for Power	What would be the impact of greater gender-balanced leadership in your organization?

2

Women in Leadership – What's Going On?

Maya attends a major sales event in Rome, an industry-wide showcase for new products with everyone from the telecoms sector present. During her time there, Maya stumbles across a networking event on women in telecoms and, intrigued by the subject matter, she decides to attend. During this session, Maya listens to the statistics on women in leadership and is amazed that the numbers globally are still so low. As the evening progresses, Maya finds herself talking to a group of women who are broadly at a similar level. As she listens to them sharing their experiences, the thing that strikes her most is how similar each story is to her own. The real eye-opener is hearing some of the women speak candidly about their desire to set up their own business and be their own boss. Maya is somewhat taken aback since up until this moment she had thought she wasn't focused enough and hadn't tried hard enough to stay on the fast track for promotion. However, as she listens to the discussion unfold and witnesses women from other continents nod in agreement when one or the other talks about missed promotions, not getting a tap on the shoulder to go for promotions, and their shock when a more junior colleague gets the position, for the first time she realizes that she is not alone. She finds herself nodding vigorously when another jokes about a recent article in the press on women's salaries being less than the men's. It cites a 10 per cent difference, but it is more like 25 per cent, exclaims the manager shaking her head in disbelief. The evening draws to a close and Maya feels as though she has experienced an epiphany. The evening has been a real eye-opener, enabling her to see that what she is experiencing is not at all unique and that there are countless others who are facing the same dilemma and considering various options. These thoughts stay with her on her long journey home.

The position of women in leadership

Understanding the global position of women in leadership is difficult primarily because there isn't a great deal of comparable data in this area. Creating benchmarks for women in leadership is critical to measuring progress and demonstrating the impact of initiatives supporting female talent. In this chapter, we discuss the most recent surveys and data demonstrating the progress of women in leadership positions and also discuss what the findings reveal to enable greater female retention and promotion.

Fifteen years after the Millennium Development Goals (MDGs) focused on targets for women in leadership, there has been substantial progress for women in leadership. At best, we will see parity achieved with our daughters who are embarking on their secondary schooling, at worst we will be lucky if our great-granddaughters achieve equality across all levels of leadership. This means there is a great deal more work to be done. This means investing effort to maintain the momentum harnessed over the last 15 years, as well as increasing efforts to speed up the process.

In 2014, the World Economic Forum produced its annual Gender Gap report, ranking countries based on how well they performed on gender-disaggregated data,[1] and this included measuring the percentage of companies with women leaders and the proportion of board positions held by women. This is a notable development, as previously gender statistics collected by the UN, World Bank, or other international agencies focused only on the presence of women in political leadership.

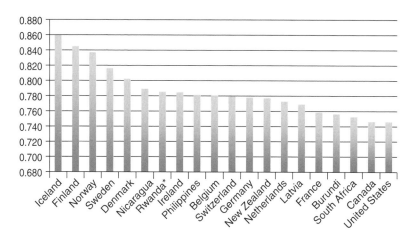

FIGURE 2.1 / Top 20 countries with the lowest gender gap

Note: (Appendix 1: Table 2.1 presents the ranking of all countries included in the report).

Figure 2.1 presents the top 20 countries, based on the World Economic Forum data.

Iceland leads the way at 0.85, followed by the Scandinavian countries. What is surprising is that the countries at the top are still some way off from absolute gender equality. Some of the countries that may surprise you by their presence in the top 20 have earned that place by virtue of a rigorous approach to engaging more women in political participation, namely Rwanda and South Africa.

The benefits of having women in senior political leadership roles are widely acknowledged: women in positions to influence key policies, ensuring that economic, financial, and employment legislation take account of the impact on women. Rwanda is a good example of the progress that can be achieved with strong and consistent representation of women in political leadership. In the 2014 Gender Gap report, Rwanda was placed seventh, ahead of countries such as Switzerland, Germany, France, Canada, and the United States (Appendix 1, Table 2.1). Rwanda has been phenomenally successful in building the presence of women in political positions and creating a strong pipeline of these women from grassroots by creating community councils with women as chairs, building their confidence to grow into their leadership roles. Rwanda is still at the beginning of its journey and there is a great deal of work needed to address gender in economic development, but with a gender-balanced political presence the country is more likely to achieve success faster and in a sustainable manner. Like Rwanda, a large number of countries have a track record of quotas for women in political roles, with varying degrees of success. Perhaps the most challenging question when we look at the impact of quotas is whether they have managed to achieve deep behavioral and attitudinal change towards women in political positions.

In 2014, we were commissioned to conduct a groundbreaking piece of work to create a report benchmarking women in leadership across the 53 Commonwealth countries.[2] The purpose of the report was to benchmark the presence of women in leadership across all sectors, in the political, private, and public sectors. Figure 2.2 ranks selected Commonwealth countries based on the proportion of board positions held by women, and Figure 2.3 ranks selected Commonwealth countries based on the proportion of women holding C-Suite roles.

Only 14 countries have a majority of their listed companies with at least one female board member (Figure 2.4). This indicates only a small section of countries have listed companies with the breadth of female representation at board level. Furthermore, when we consider the proportion of board and C-Suite women in countries with 100 listed companies again only a small number of countries are close to the 30 per cent benchmark for women in leadership in the corporate sector (Figure 2.5).

We see a relatively similar pattern for women on the boards and holding C-Suite roles in countries with smaller stock exchanges (Figure 2.6). There are some countries that have reached and exceeded the 30 per cent benchmark for women at corporate level (Botswana and Jamaica).[7]

If we consider the position of women in the public sector, we see there is better performance in terms of the number of women on board positions in state-owned enterprises (see Figure 2.7).

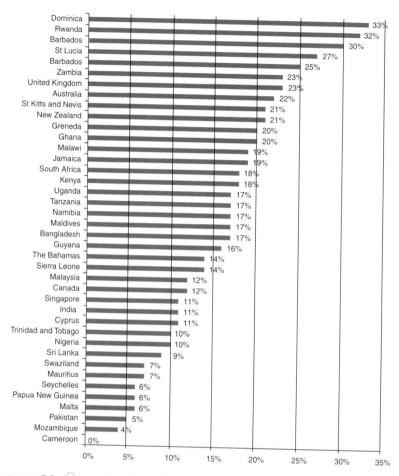

FIGURE 2.2 / Proportion of board positions held by women in selected Commonwealth countries[3]

The overview of Commonwealth countries shows strong trends of women in public sector leadership in the Caribbean and African states. The Asian countries, in contrast, do not have the same proportion of women in senior leadership positions, and none of these countries have reached 20 per cent of female representation on public sector boards.

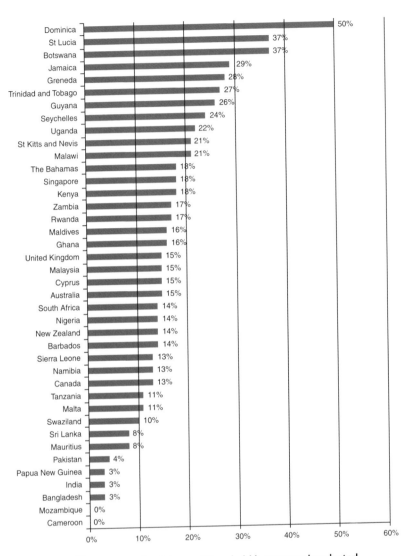

FIGURE 2.3 Proportion of C-Suite positions held by women in selected Commonwealth countries[4]

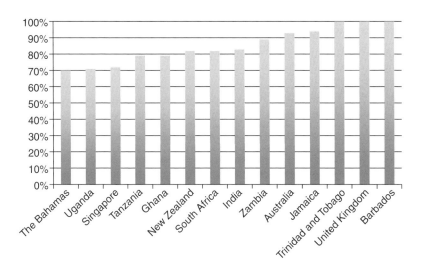

FIGURE 2.4 / Countries where at least 70 per cent of listed companies have at least one female board member[5]

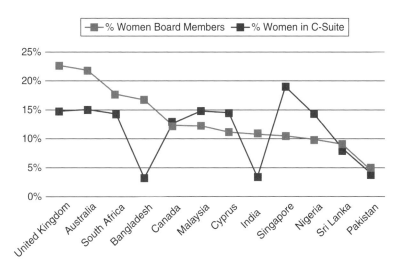

FIGURE 2.5 / Proportion of board and C-Suite women in countries with 100 listed companies[6]

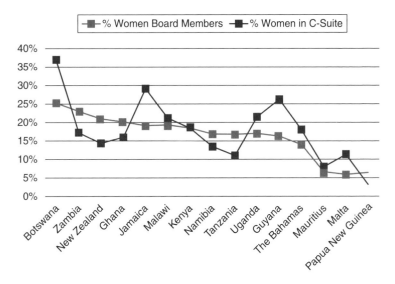

FIGURE 2.6 / **Proportion of women holding board positions in countries with smaller stock exchanges, 99 or fewer listed companies**[8]

The discussion around women on boards of both corporate and state-owned enterprises (SOEs) has been dominated by debates on quotas.[10] The discussion usually focuses on the merits of quotas for boards and simplifies the complexity of the situation to a carrot and stick approach. Quotas take on different forms, they can take the form of legislated or voluntary targets. When legislated, there will be sanctions for non-compliance in the form of fines, for example. They can be binding and permanent or temporary; the latter are described as sunset quotas and quotas can also be used to target certain areas where traditionally there has been a deficit of female presence, either in the private or public sector.

Working in the Commonwealth community has given us access to a broad cross-section of countries that have differing economic, social, and cultural structures, as well as very different legislative frameworks around gender equality and employment. There are a small number of countries in the Commonwealth that have legislated quotas for women on corporate boards; India, Malaysia, South Africa, Kenya. None of these countries

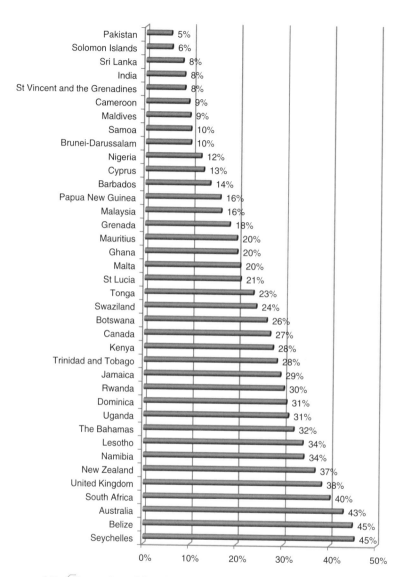

FIGURE 2.7 Proportion of female board members in state-owned enterprises[9]

had reached their targets at the time of writing. Countries that had a strong history of gender equality and legislation to protect gender equality had progressed considerably in the public sector but had not reached the 30 per cent critical mass of women in private sector leadership.

We wanted to understand more clearly what factors stopped women from gaining senior leadership roles; was it about education and women not having access to the right levels of formal education? Was it about political empowerment – ensuring women had the ability to participate in political decision-making? Was it about economic participation – ensuring women were able to engage in economic activity? We looked at each of these considerations; the categories identified by the World Economic Forum (Table 2 in Appendix 1) and measured by correlation how they impacted the presence of women on boards according to each Commonwealth region.

Asia demonstrated a strong correlation between infrastructure factors and the participation of women on boards. By contrast, in Africa the infrastructure does not seem to have a correlation with the participation of women on boards. In the Caribbean the infrastructure factors were found to have a moderate correlation with participation of women on boards. We omitted Europe as it only contained three (Commonwealth) countries, and within the Pacific region only New Zealand and Australia had usable data so these two regions have been omitted from this analysis. The overall findings indicate there are factors beyond infrastructure that drive the participation of women on boards. The data from Asia demonstrates that infrastructure is necessary to create the pipeline of female talent. However, the lack of critical mass of women on boards in any Asian countries would indicate that infrastructure alone is not enough to get women onto boards in a sizeable manner – there needs to be something else.

As we review the findings in this report, we are starting to build a clearer picture of what the situation is for women in leadership. The infrastructure, by which we mean education, political and economic empowerment, and health provisions, are clearly important building blocks to ensure women are skilled and able to actively engage in their communities. Quotas have been effective in galvanizing women into leadership positions; but they do present a mixed result as companies may recruit women who are not ready for board positions in a rush to avoid fines, or even worse, companies may simply decide to budget for the fines. Norway is a great success story demonstrating the impact of quotas in getting women into senior leadership positions. Getting women onto boards is only half the story. There is also an important emphasis on ensuring a similar number of positions continue to be held by women in the future. A recent piece of research by Sucheta Nadkarni and Elaine Oon at Cambridge University demonstrated how quotas are important in getting women into senior roles.[11] They found that while quotas did have the desired effect in increasing numbers, they were less effective in keeping women on boards over the longer term. Their research found provisions within companies and cultural nuances were more important in determining the presence of women in board positions.

For the purposes of this book, the evidence is really important in identifying what is going to make the difference when countries and companies invest in supporting gender diversity for leadership. All of the investment in infrastructure is essential to create a level playing field, but we have identified three additional factors:

- The nature of the relationship between three groups – government, women's advocacy groups, and corporate/organizations.
- The culture of organizations to create an environment to promote and support gender diversity.
- Championing relationships, creating one-to-one relationships to actively promote female talent.

A word about our case studies

We wanted to ensure the ideas we were developing could be applied to women in different countries as well as different sectors and types of organizations. We formally interviewed 60 women in 55 different countries. Over a period of eight months we interviewed women across time zones from Canada to Singapore, Botswana to Malta, from Latvia to Bangladesh. We were keen to find the most diverse range of women leaders. This meant using different types of companies, public and private sector organizations, charities, entrepreneurial start-ups, and family firms. The women we included in the research had been identified by us or by colleagues as pioneers in their fields, leaders; many held formal positions such as former heads of state, government officials, corporate and public sector board members, C-Suite roles, as well as founders of entrepreneurial organizations that had grown to be significant players in their fields.

As we analyzed the profiles of the women we had interviewed, we identified certain elements these cases shared, which undoubtedly had a direct impact on their achievements. These stories of women who have achieved senior leadership roles, and in many cases have been pioneers, demonstrate the breadth of women who shared a similar experience in their leadership journeys – that of being championed. The diverse range of voices in this book reinforce the importance of championing as the means by which women can build and achieve their leadership aspirations.

We are privileged to work in the field of women's leadership training and development in companies across the world, from large multinational companies to public sector organizations, from entrepreneurial start-ups to multi-generational family businesses. Time and again we find women leaders who share great stories of tenacity and resilience. The consistent message in this book is the presence of championing as a means of promoting this extraordinary female talent. The international dimension of the book allows us to demonstrate how championing is applied in a range of different contexts where cultural and social conditions create challenges to gender equality.

Tasks

For individuals:

- How do you feel about your career progress to date?
- Are you satisfied with your rate of progress?
- What are the top three factors driving change in your sector?

What are the top three factors driving change?	What does this mean for me? Opportunities or challenges?
1.	
2.	
3.	

For organizations:

- What data does your organization record on the promotion of women at various leadership levels?
- How does your company compare with the industry average?
- How available is this information?

What are the top three demographic trends that will impact your recruitment?

Trends	Impact on recruitment in the organization?
1.	
2.	
3.	

3

Barriers to Progress: Confidence and Bias

In the canteen, Maya happened to sit down for coffee with someone whose face she recognized, but whom she couldn't quite identify. As they started talking, Maya suddenly remembered; this was the VP of Marketing, Dara Swann, who normally worked out of the California office. Dara was charming and interested, and got Maya to tell her story. Liking what she heard and saw, she researched Maya's track record when she got back to her office. Within two weeks, having spoken with Maya's boss, she suggested Maya tried for a new job: why don't you come and work in my department for a while, I really need someone with your experience. It will be a big step up. Maya was flattered, but said no – there was too much on her plate, she didn't feel ready for such a big change and she hoped the opportunity would arise again when she would be better prepared.

What are some of the underlying reasons for women's lack of progress into leadership positions around the world, compared to men? Having acknowledged the pace of change is too slow (see Chapter 1) we wanted to understand what underpins this lag. We are constantly engaging with women in our programs and through our research have asked many hundreds to identify what they feel gets in the way of achieving leadership roles. We also read and consulted widely and mapped what we had discovered against what others had found, both in relation to what works to help women and what stood in their way.

We do not wish to lay out long lists of possible reasons and possible solutions in this book but rather to focus on what we found to be most important, to explore areas where action can be taken with effective results and where there is evidence that good practice has actually worked, and changed things on the ground – in women's lived experiences, not just in policy and rhetoric.

Barriers and boosts

When we asked successful women what they perceived as the barriers to *their own* progress, they came up with a relatively short list: needing more assertiveness about their career progression, more transparency in recruitment/promotion processes, unfriendly organizational cultures, and, compared to men, a lack of pull-through from senior leaders. As Jane Dennis from Malta reflects: "If I'm honest: I don't think being female was an obstacle itself, I don't think people would look at you and think you couldn't do something. But higher up there was something about social exclusion." Hasnah Omar from Malaysia shared her views: "There is still a perception about women in the corporate world and I believe it is partly due to the 'Old Boys' mentality that still persists, in that generally those in the corporate world feel more comfortable dealing with people they know who happen to be wearing pants. Board and gender diversity has a long journey still. We have to keep on working on this, otherwise we may not be heard."

But when we asked women what they felt the barriers were for women in general, and examined the literature in depth, two fundamental themes emerged. Firstly, we saw that even when opportunities were created, women were, on average, less inclined to put themselves forward than the men around them, which can be attributed to having less self-belief, or confidence.[1] We called this hesitation.

We also saw that the "playing field" was far from level: there were innate biases, which were largely cross-cultural, that prevented fair and meritocratic decisions being made at the most fundamental levels. We found that even when women did put themselves forward, they were not judged according to the same criteria as men. And that this was as true when they were girls at school as when they were middle managers at work.

What we also discovered initially from our own experiences, and later through our work, was that, when women said they were invisible, that was true in some circumstances: they were not being seen or heard, even when "their hands were waving." We often saw a woman make a valid intervention in a meeting or group discussion, which was ignored until later repeated by a man, whereupon it was acknowledged and even

"That's an excellent suggestion, Miss Triggs. Perhaps one of
the men here would like to make it."

FIGURE 3.1 / "Miss Triggs" cartoon

Source:© PUNCH Magazine, 1988, Riana Duncan.

praised. It happened to us, our colleagues, our friends, our research sub-
jects, and coaching clients.

These were manifestations of fundamental human sub-conscious bias, not
just a "female problem." Bias was not only a phenomenon in individuals,
but something that was both influenced by, and contributed significantly
to, organizational culture. Sub-conscious biases led to women being
denied opportunities because of assumptions about their capabilities and
competence, which people – both men and women – were not aware of
harboring.

Lack of confidence is another factor. This shows up in a number of
ways; Katty Kay and Claire Shipman for example, cited research that
demonstrates that men initiate salary negotiations four times as often as
women.[2] A lack of confidence seemed to us to be the underlying reason
for other barriers: women's tendency towards self-limiting beliefs and
behaviors, which sometimes led to hesitating about or refusing to take up
challenging opportunities for growth, and therefore missing out on the
chance to develop confidence.

So we decided to look in more depth at the differences between men
and women, as well as women's confidence and potential bias against
women, and their effects.

Is there a *real* difference?

Women consistently appear to be less confident than men. This compara-
tive lack of confidence is widely recognized as one of the greatest challenges faced by women,[3] and it can only be tackled when we understand
it better and recognize how much it gets in the way of our progress. We
know that men and women are more similar than they are different, but
still they are different. For example, women and men differ in how they
respond to stress. Women are more prone to anxiety than men, but much
less likely to commit suicide,[4] and less prone to most diseases.[5] Women
have a greater tendency to focus and dwell on negative, rather than positive feedback.[6] Women are more sociable, appearing more sensitive to

their social context, and to what others think of them, but less likely to use aggression to solve problems.[7]

We know more now than we did even ten years ago about some of the reasons for differences between men and women, *on average*. Appendix 2 provides a summary of some of the underlying brain-based differences: not just relating to brain structures, but also to the differences in connections and chemistry. Neuroscience is just at the foothills of revealing some of the processes that underpin behavior. The more we know, the more we see how little we know of the complexity and interdependence of the whole system that is the brain and the body. With all these caveats it is understandable that very little so far has been proven as to the biological underpinnings of differences between the genders. Research results are contradictory and controversial, with little consensus. For some people, even to acknowledge that there might be fundamental gender-based differences in the brain can be a politicized neurosexist minefield. Remember the controversy Larry Summers, then President of Harvard, caused in 2005 when he suggested that women might have, on average, less innate mathematical capability than men?

Being aware of the complexities should help us steer clear of facile judgments based on "what everyone knows." So what can we say – if anything – meaningfully, that will genuinely help us understand gender diversity and exploit its potential value in a range of social and work environments? And what does this mean in terms of how we see women? Is lack of confidence an innate hindrance for women's progress and is it exacerbated by male-dominated environments? And can women be leaders just as well as men if they are less confident? We don't believe women need to be "fixed," but having heard from so many women that *they* feel they need more confidence, might confidence be the one area where we think something does need to be addressed?

Confidence

Confidence is not fearlessness and not courage. It is more akin to trust – trusting yourself, a feeling that you are more likely to succeed than fail in any future action. It is therefore not just a function of our chemical and genetic make-up but also of our life experiences. A track record of successful actions develops confidence: you are more likely to believe that you will succeed in a future endeavor if you have succeeded in the past. For example, if that successful action is landing a ball in a net, getting a yes to a request for extra budget on the phone, completing a project on time to the satisfaction of a client, raising a child, writing a compelling report, you are building your own track record of success. Our past experiences with various tasks and achievements, and the feedback from these as to our success or failure, help determine our levels of confidence. Sometimes that feedback is intrinsic to the action and immediate: a ball in the net is quick and easy to spot. Feedback from other kinds of activities is harder to gauge. For example, the impact of what we say in a speech, or even the impact of our appearance on another person, might take time to emerge or we may never quite understand it. Behaviors where the outcomes are not obvious can be difficult to judge. At these times, past failures, or a tendency to anxiety or pessimism, or feedback of the wrong kind from others can create or reinforce that little nagging voice in our own heads that tells us that wasn't good enough.

Albert Bandura's theory of self-efficacy,[8] that is, the extent to which you believe you can complete tasks and achieve goals, is another lens through which we can look at self-confidence and the elements that combine to create that mental state. Self-efficacy is correlated with the sense that you are in control of your life and that your own actions, decisions, and persistence play more of a role in shaping your life than random external factors or luck. A sense of self-efficacy helps manage risk and fear of uncertainty. People who believe that their motivation and actions will determine their outcomes are more likely to put more effort into succeeding, and thus also are more likely to perform well. Believing that other forces are more powerful may lead to inactivity and despondency, and a tendency not to try hard, or not to try at all. Again, like confidence, the sense of self-efficacy is built up over time by our actions and how we and others interpret their outcomes and feedback from them. Success breeds the sense of being effective and in control. Michele Goldman from Australia shares her views on the transient nature of confidence: "Once you lose your sense of self-confidence, believing in yourself, you can't draw on your internal, personal resources to get things done. You need to believe in yourself."

Confidence is a complex state

Both men and women can appear confident and yet be feeling anything but. They can be confident in one sphere, but not in another. For example, they may be confident in getting a team to complete a project on time and to budget, but feel very anxious about presenting their results to the Board. Or they may be confident in high-level negotiations but doubt their own abilities as a parent, home alone with two fractious toddlers. We heard many stories of people who act confidently, but only after immense effort to overcome feelings of self-doubt. Even the most powerful global leaders experience self-doubt at some time, as illustrated by Christine Lagarde, Managing Director of the International Monetary Fund, and Angela Merkel, Chancellor of Germany, who both describe how their perfectionist tendencies result in over-preparation for key meetings, a habit Lagarde has described as emerging from a need to ensure nothing goes wrong, no mistakes are made: "there are still moments when I have to go deep inside myself and pull my strength, confidence, background, history, experience and all the rest of it, to assert a particular point."[9]

We understand that women suffer more than men from imposter or fraud syndrome,[10] that feeling that even if you are at the top of your profession, even if you have run a FTSE 100 company, or been voted the top international prize for Physics, that little voice chips away saying "one day you will be found out." This behavior, described as "imposter phenomenon" was attributed to women by Pauline Clance.[11] Imposter syndrome has been studied in student and academic populations and has been linked with high achievers and perfectionists, and unsurprisingly it has been also been linked to having parents with high expectations.

When women do break through to senior ranks, even after they have learned to own their achievements and how to bring them appropriately to others' attention, there is often still a sense of uncertainty, of lack of confidence deeply hidden in many of them, even after years at the top. It constantly shocks us when we see so many women consciously under-playing their success in a way that almost seems like self-sabotage. We are not saying that this is a universal trait, and we know many women who are exceptions to this rule. But a large number of women do feel as though they do not "deserve to be where they are" – at least some of the time, and some of them allow those feelings to show clearly.

Confidence appears to be a state that needs to be constantly reinforced, through the results of our actions. Not taking an opportunity, not try-ing something new, is potentially damaging to the ability to develop your confidence.[12] Working in environments in which your initiatives and actions are constantly being frustrated or blocked can induce or reinforce a lack of trust in your own abilities. One of our coaching clients was responsible for IP commercialization in a research-intensive institu-tion. Constantly frustrated by restrictive policies that limited what could be done with IP, or that just caused inordinate delays, she began to lose motivation and to feel that it was her own lack of ability to attract invest-ment that was the problem. She eventually left the organization to head up a successful consultancy.

The role of testosterone

Testosterone, known as the male hormone, creates the conditions for the main male physical characteristics, early in the life of a foetus in the womb and then again at puberty. Both men and women secrete testos-terone, but men on average have about 8–10 times more than women. Testosterone is positively correlated with characteristically male behav-iors such as aggression and risk taking, but also with confidence (see Appendix 2). In humans, levels of testosterone alone are not enough to predict dominance, or leadership, and too much testosterone leads to excessive risk taking and aggression. It is too simplistic to blame the lack of female leaders, or even women's lack of confidence, on this one hormone. It may play an important role, but so does the ability to manage stress, to be resilient, and above all to exercise self-control – to be able to manage our attention and our emotions.[13] As we explain in Chapter 8, there is much more to leadership – and we will be talking about how to boost testosterone too.

I was lucky

An indicator of women's lack of confidence in their abilities is that they have a tendency to describe their leadership position and achievements as being down to luck rather than their own actions. When you ask a woman about her success, what it is that got her into a senior leadership role, she will mention her hard work, the role her colleagues played, the support of a boss or partner, possibly even her skills and expertise, and then undermine those by adding "I was lucky," "I was in the right place at the right time," or a similar phrase. During the course of our work with women, if we had a dollar for every time we had heard that statement from a senior, successful, outwardly confident woman we could go on several luxury holidays!

There is a disconnect between attributing our own success to luck but the success of others to their abilities and to a fair system. The conflict is evident in women who resolutely refuse to promote their achievements at work, believing that one day their work will be noticed by a "Prince" of a senior manager – some time, somewhere – who will seek them out and fit the glass slipper of promotion on their perfectly formed foot! Kitty describes this as the Cinderella syndrome,[14] a mindset amongst women in the workplace who feel their hard work will be recognized and rewarded by others around them, and that therefore they do not need to "blow their own trumpet."

At the same time, we do not often hear women attributing *lack* of career progress to luck. Instead, they tend to own their mistakes or shortcomings more easily than their successes. There is widespread evidence that women are more self-critical than men when it comes to appearance, but in our work we have seen that to be the case for other attributes and actions as well. It is as though they will accept that they are responsible for what goes wrong, but not for what goes right in their lives. One senior woman gave us five or six negative beliefs about herself in the first hour of our first meeting; for example, "I am no good at statistics," "my analysis is weak," "I am not influential enough." And she had no idea that she was being openly self-denigrating. Some of her statements, when probed, were demonstrably untrue – for example, her ability to analyze statistics and come up with meaningful recommendations was excellent and a core part of her work. Our own beliefs can have such an enormous impact on what we do and how we are perceived. Champions can help us become aware of habits of self-critical beliefs and also help us challenge them.

Whenever we challenge women to think about how they have presented themselves, and we call them out on talking about their "luck,"[15] they stop and really consider what has enabled them to succeed in their chosen profession, to reach senior leadership roles. Once these women step back and reflect on their leadership narrative, they acknowledge that in so many cases luck had very little to do with their success, and their new story includes the lyrics, *"The harder I work, the luckier I get!"*[16]

From our interviews and work with women, we have concluded that, for many women, attributing their success to luck is a conscious or even unconscious way of not appearing boastful.[17] It provides a way to avoid standing out, perhaps to protect them from being seen as pushy. We recognize the challenges when a girl or woman is regarded as bossy. The connotations are never positive. Yet for us, there is something so crushing when we see women who have achieved so much and yet they won't even own the label of being "successful." Only when this behavior is challenged do the women realize what they are doing.

Some women genuinely see their career successes as not due to their own efforts, but as a result of some external force. This may be attributable in some cases to cultural or even religious factors, but even so there is still room for human capabilities in the equation. In other cases it may be more to do with a sense that they are not in control of their lives; other people, or the environment around them more generally, the systems and processes in which they operate, are shaping the outcomes of what they do more than they are. This is different to a belief in fate or a deity that determines the future. When challenged, these women often have to think very hard before acknowledging that yes, perhaps their own skills and actions had contributed something to their success.

Hesitation and self-limitation

As we saw earlier, a lack of confidence can also lead to self-limiting beliefs and behaviors that in turn reinforce the lack of confidence. Some women appear reluctant to put themselves in situations where they could fail, more so because they are worried about letting other people down. The classic example of women looking at a job description and not applying because they do not meet all the criteria fully has been demonstrated as true again and again. Where men will "have a go," women will hesitate. Both Kitty and Shaheena can point to painful examples in their own lives. Kitty vividly remembers not filling in a form for accreditation as a photographer by the UK's Motorsport Association because she did not have the "right" length of experience and number of publications. It took a racing driver friend – a male – to persuade her that it did not really matter … and she became an MSA photographer.

Saying no to opportunity

When that light finally shines on you and you are offered an exciting and challenging new opportunity, what happens? You may jump into that role, arms open and full of enthusiasm. Well done! You are a member of a small but important group – that of role models for others. Many women, however, will push back on opportunities, with so many valid and a number of less valid reasons: "It's not the right time, I am not ready yet." "Family commitments mean I can't travel, or move to a new city or country." "I don't have the skills set or experience to take on this new role." "I want to start a family and I don't think I'll have time."

There are always very good reasons why you can't take that next role and you are the author of many of those reasons. Shaheena remembers that when she returned to work five months after her first son was born, she had just completed her PhD and was invited to attend a number of overseas conferences. She always managed to find a good reason not to go. This became a pattern of self-sabotage. However, a conversation with an individual who was championing her into these international opportunities helped her to realize the impact this was likely to have on her career. When her second son was born three years later, she was committed to overseas trips and even took him to a conference in Bahrain when he was four months old – he was the youngest delegate in the session!

Having spoken to many women we heard stories of a similar nature. Is this something you have witnessed amongst friends or colleagues or closer to your own experience? You have rehearsed the arguments against taking that big step over and over again. In amongst these reactions, you may remember how hard you have worked, how much you have invested into building your career, how much value you add and yet you still manage to convince yourself you shouldn't take the next step. Why? Do you think you are not ready for it, or that you may drop one of the balls you are juggling?

Women hit a vicious cycle – you believe you can't "do it" so you don't step up and you end up limiting yourself. You then become disillusioned or bored with your current job. You become dissatisfied as you see peers being promoted and realize that a part of you knows you could do a much better job. But did you give the message that you are not in the "game"? Or were you reflecting what you imagined others might have been thinking and "living down to" their expectations? Your family, friends, work colleagues, and the media are all powerful players in communicating expectations, and how you listen to them matters.

A female CEO of a communications company based in Southern Europe has seen the results of self-limitation. Reflecting on these experiences, she said, "When I do coach women coming back, I do see the conflict and compromise. I would say, don't compromise for work that doesn't attract you and give you energy. Some women step back and take lesser roles because they want to ring-fence time with their kids. But if you are not stretched by what you do at work, that is where it goes wrong ... you are choosing the worst of both worlds."

Indeed, companies are increasingly recognizing the importance of giving women who return from maternity leave "meatier roles," and in doing so giving them a chance to feel valued.

Later in this book, we discuss the importance of talent management for senior leaders. If a senior executive is going to promote an individual they want to back a winner, someone who is hungry for a challenge, who can deliver on their promises and fulfill their potential. If they offer an opportunity and a woman turns it down, even once, this can reinforce stereotypes. We have heard time and again senior male executives telling us that they know women are less ambitious than men, that they want to spend more time with the family. We have also had clients tell us they see pregnant women "checking out" of the workplace before they have gone on maternity leave. These behaviors do reinforce stereotypes and make it even harder for the next group of women coming through the organizations. This adds to what Stephen Sidebottom from Standard Chartered calls the "waterfall" effect,[18] with high attrition rates of women at middle and senior levels. And yet women tell us that they are ambitious; that they want these opportunities, but that they are not being offered them. It may be that spotting talent or even building confidence are not enough. More proactive initiatives are needed – like championing. The language used for job descriptions and the way opportunities might be presented may need to work better for women too.

Bias

Whether we like it or not, all humans, men and women, are affected by biases, most of which they are not aware of harboring. This does not mean we are bad people, but that bias is an evolutionary relic that is an inappropriate response to our current environment. What this means is that some of the shortcuts the brain takes, to help us make those rapid decisions that millennia ago worked well to help keep us alive, are no longer valid or useful. Making a judgment about someone who walks into your space depending on how much like you or not like you they look might have saved a Neanderthal from being killed by a Homo sapien or vice-versa, but it is less useful in a modern office environment. Daniel Kahneman presents a long and varied list of biases,[19] and some contribute significantly to how men and women are perceived differently. For example, "confirmation bias" inclines us to pay attention only to those inputs that easily fit into our previously held views. They allow us to interpret what we see and hear so that it confirms what we already think. For example, in a meeting, we are adamant that the only woman spoke a lot more than any of the men, whereas a recording of the same meeting will show she spoke a lot less. And we will firmly believe that our subjective experience is the right one, IF we believe that women, on the whole, are garrulous compared to men – and women are just as likely to hold that biased perspective as men. We are more likely to think someone is authoritative if they have a low voice. Margaret Thatcher, the first British female Prime Minister, who remained in office from 1979 to 1990, was trained to develop a lower pitch when talking. The same is true for taller people; the research team led by Gert Stulp in 2012 found that taller US Presidential candidates were more likely to be victorious, as their height created the perception of the candidates having greater leadership and communication skills.[20] Culturally-determined expectations and stereotypes also play a very significant role and it is not always possible to easily disentangle them from bias.

Individuals and organizations will vehemently deny bias, because they are not aware of it. However, the evidence is now overwhelming: men and women doing the same tasks in the same way in the same roles are judged differently because our cultural and evolutionarily-defined views and expectations of them are different. It is an archetypal double bind: if a woman succeeds by using the same behavior as a man, she is seen as aggressive, pushy, and unlikeable.[21] If she puts emphasis on being liked, and helping others rather than delivering results herself, she is seen as lacking competence. And, if she keeps her achievements quiet, she is overlooked or not seen as leadership material. Sheryl Sandberg made this point very effectively in *Lean In*, in her chapter on Success and Likeability: "When a woman excels at her job, both male and female co-workers will remark that she may be accomplishing a lot but is 'not as well liked as her peers'. She is probably also 'too aggressive', 'not a team player', 'a bit political', 'can't be trusted' or 'difficult'."[22]

Men and women use different language to describe the same behavior in men and women. How often have you heard an assertive very senior male manager described as bossy or pushy? Or described as selfish for not spending more time at home looking after the children? An advertisement for Pantene made in the Philippines in 2013 made that point beautifully.[23] A study conducted by Kieran Snyder for Fortune.com, and reported by Kathleen Davis in Fast Company in August 2014,[24] found that the word "abrasive" was never used about men in 248 performance reviews – only about women.

A very interesting study by Kristen Schilt found that comparing the experiences of transgender people, male to female and female to male, was a robust way of testing for bias.[25] In many cases, those who had changed gender were in exactly the same or very similar jobs. One female to male biologist found that, as a male, he was treated with more respect, he was taken more seriously, and his statements were not questioned but accepted. And this difference seemed to be common across the majority of female to male transgenders.[26] The opposite seemed to be the case for male to female transgendered people: their views were doubted more easily and they were not assumed to be competent unless they proved it.

Naaz Coker, Non-Executive Director for the National Audit Office and a Trustee for the Royal College for Obstetricians and Gynaecologists, based in the UK, describes the broader barriers that still impact women: "It hasn't shifted – I see as many prejudices now as I did 30 years ago. The difference is women fight more, we have shifted it but not as much as I would have expected."

Another study, reported in the *The Economist* in January 2015,[27] showed that where judgments about people are based on cultural beliefs that cannot be easily proven or disproven (for example, that mathematical ability is based on innate talent), they are more likely to be biased – against both women and racial minorities – and women and minorities are likely to share these biases. There have also been many studies showing that when gender or racial information (such as names or photos) are stripped out from applications, judgments are different to when they are available. Others have shown that an application form for a job or PhD opportunity with a woman's name attached is judged more harshly than with a male name, even if the applications are identical.[28]

Bias could be stronger in environments where there is considerable internal competition. Such competition increases fear – of loss of status or even of your job, of loss of face, of shame. This may create a sense of enmity, of us and them, which in turn may strengthen a biased perspective against others. This perspective may be one reason why women often feel uncomfortable working in highly competitive environments, especially if they are in a minority. It is not just the competitiveness and any aggressive behavior that results from this, it is that the bias against them increases.[29]

Impact of early experience

Early experiences matter – whether directly through our own experiences or, as Bandura argues, by observing others (hence the importance of accessible role models).[30] These experiences shape our brain, our personality, and our view of ourselves. Parents, carers, close relatives, and family friends who – driven by biases of which they are unaware, or conscious social stereotypes – treat girls and boys differently in terms of the breadth of testing experiences and levels of responsibility, can set up attitudes and behaviors that may be unhelpful in later life. Social stereotypes and biases can be reinforced: for example, girls who are not expected to do well at math and sciences may internalize that expectation.

Over-protected girls who are not allowed age-appropriate autonomy in decisions about their activities or friends may find it difficult to accept later that they are responsible for their own progress and their own mistakes. Girls who are praised and rewarded for being good – that is, obedient, quiet and hard-working – might find it difficult to stand up for themselves and ask for a raise in their later career. How parents deal with failure and transgression is also important. Are the rules the same for girls and boys in the family? Are girls expected to be good, so that "naughtiness" is less tolerated, whereas in boys the same behavior might be seen as natural boyish rough and tumble and risk taking?

In school, the rules are clear and compliance with the rules brings public approval, if not always sustained attention. This pattern builds expectations that we will be recognized and rewarded for good work, we will be rewarded for waiting our turn to speak and for not being disruptive or attention-seeking. This can lead to Cinderella Syndrome, as discussed earlier, where we expect good work to be recognized and rewarded, without additional effort on our part to bring it to the attention of others. We feel uncomfortable if we have to bring our achievements to the attention of those above us, blowing our own trumpet. Perhaps we did not notice that noise and disruption actually garnered more attention, or, if we did, decided that that kind of attention was "not for us." Another factor may be that girls and women are uncomfortable with being or appearing competitive with their peers, or that they are competing in a different way to boys and men … competing by being the best at obeying the rules, rather than looking at how to compete on results.

One of our most able coachees, a woman running a medium-sized country for a major technology multinational, put it like this when we encouraged her to ask assertively for the promotion for which she'd been overlooked three times: "I can't do it; boasting isn't me, it goes against everything I believe in. The quality of my work should be recognized." Yet this does not happen: time and again so many women find they have been overlooked, making them feel invisible in the organization, regardless of their achievements. We acknowledge that assertiveness does not always come easily, even to confident and able women. It needs practice to know what you are promoting and how you will present it appropriately to others.

Claire, based in Malta, describes how women are likely to react to these situations: "I try not to link this to gender but, for example, if I go with something firm and assertive to my boss he will snap and swear and belittle me, so I distance myself and I go with a certain tone and level of voice … so yes, I can see a need to assert myself."

We discuss the role of teachers as champions in the next chapter, but at this point we want to emphasize the importance of educators as powerful forces in shaping experience and stereotype-based expectations. According to Susan Harter, evidence shows that teachers do perceive girls to be more compliant and prosocial than boys in the classroom.[31] A report published in March 2015 by the OECD showed that girls are now significantly outstripping boys at school. The report attributes this in part to girls' spending more time on homework, their superior enjoyment of reading (boys prefer to play). The author also argues this may also emerge from the "bias" of (mostly female) teachers who prefer children who are "polite, eager and stay out of fights." Teachers have little incentive to offer challenging experiences to girls, where they can try out appropriate risky behaviors in a controlled environment. They are too busy trying to manage behaviors in larger classes. Of course, within the curriculum there are opportunities to challenge and test students, for example in sports, but there is evidence that more girls than boys are reluctant to engage in physical and competitive activity.[32]

So the combination of the tendency to be less confident, together with sub-conscious bias and generations of social gender stereotyping, can be damaging and create a lasting vicious cycle.

In this chapter, we have navigated our way through the reasons why women hesitate in the workplace – underpinning the reasons why championing is such a powerful resource. We recognize there are significant social and cultural differences that will influence behavior, but we also see similar patterns of bias across regions and even sectors. Imagine what your world would look like without these barriers, the self-limiting behaviors, or the biases. Imagine what opportunities would open up for you, your daughters, and granddaughters and how the timeframe for gender parity in the workplace could rapidly decrease.

Tasks

For individuals:

Preparation is the key!

Next time you are going into a situation where you feel you would like to be more confident, for example, a difficult client meeting or an interview, try the following techniques.

Write down the top three achievements over the last year or two that you are most proud of – at work, at home, personally, or through your hobbies. Remember how you felt when you achieved them.

My achievements	My strengths from these achievements

Just before you are due to go into a difficult situation (ideally within 15 minutes of it), find a private space where you won't be interrupted (either your office or the ladies toilet) and hold a power pose for two minutes – see the Amy Cuddy Ted Talk "Your body language shapes who you are."[33]

For organizations:

What diversity and inclusion (D&I) policies or processes are in place to help redress sub-conscious bias? How well do you and your colleagues know about them?

What other measures could be implemented that would specifically help you?

What can you do to share these ideas – do you have a women's network, or a diversity lead you can talk to?

4

Why Championing Works So Well for Women

Maya's champion, Dara, has moved on to another company as COO. A year later, she contacts Maya out of the blue to ask her to apply for a new job. It is a significant promotion with frontline responsibility managing partner relations. Again Maya's first answer is no. She is worried about all the travel involved and the change in responsibilities makes her anxious about her ability to deliver. But this time Dara does not take no for an answer. Her company is growing fast, partners are key for established and new markets and she needs someone with both the right skills and a track record of delivering results. She knows Maya is empathetic and reliable, with a strategic perspective of the industry, and that she will shine in a new, supportive environment. Dara is persuasive and offers her a flexible package – Maya accepts. Six months later, she says I LOVE my job – she is happy to be back on the fast track and the flexibility means that although she does travel a lot, she also works from home a lot and sees more of her family.

When we asked successful women to tell us what it was that most helped them reach significant leadership positions in their careers, there were three common factors in almost all their stories: the first was having people in their lives who believed in them, who opened their eyes to their own worth and potential, and opened doors for them. The second was having a wide range of experiences with significant responsibility early on in their careers, if not in their lives. And finally, the one factor that emerged again and again, in different guises, was confidence. As one of our respondents stated: "I had an unbelievable Head at my girls' school. She said that one day a woman would be President and it never occurred to me that I couldn't do anything."

When we asked these women about the barriers they encountered in their leadership journeys, almost all of the women paused and then responded along the lines of – barriers? What barriers? "I didn't see any barriers," one woman told us, "I only saw opportunities."

But when we asked them what they thought held *other* women back, they confirmed what our original research had revealed, a short list of barriers clustered around a lack of confidence and internal and external biases, as we explained in Chapter 3. They also acknowledged some of the barriers were not evident until they were further into their careers, as described by Amelia, a senior consultant: "I did not experience any discrimination in my early career. I was in a male-oriented environment but fitted in well and didn't think I had any barriers in front of me. But by the time I was in my 30s and had been promoted, I seemed to always be in meetings, with few or no other women, where my views were not taken seriously. I was sometimes dismissed as too emotional or abrasive, and did not feel as valued as the men around me."

And when we mapped these three success factors against the barriers, we had an "AHA!" moment. We can still feel, as we write, the tingle of realizing what we had discovered. **This** is why championship throughout life, and at work, has such an amazing effect: it redresses the confidence balance and enables women to address bias! Confidence allows women to overcome hesitation so as to take up opportunities and even create them from scratch. Confidence enables women to stretch their potential and to learn how to manage their reactions to risk. Confidence gives women the desire to take on challenges and responsibilities. And increasing confidence also allows women to tackle bias head on – in themselves and others. Championing provides the missing link that enables women to build this confidence through the following experiences:

1. Attempt challenging opportunities over time with appropriate support and succeed in a majority of them, growing in scale.
2. Have access to successful female role models and observe them in action and even have the chance to work with them in close proximity.
3. Experience positive "feedforward" about their capacity for future success, so increasing their appetite for new opportunities.
4. Challenge bias in themselves and others.
5. Challenge self-limiting beliefs and hesitation through evidence of their own success.
6. Build their resilience and their ability to handle failure and the negative feedback.
7. Benefit from interacting with an individual who enthusiastically believes in them.

The championing relationship that encompasses all of these elements creates the strongest foundation for leadership success.

And we knew we had something very real. We had identified a pattern throughout our work which was fully supported in these interviews. A champion creates the right circumstances for successful actions that increase confidence for the "one to watch" (OTW).

Champions challenge biases in organizations beyond an individual level, by setting the example of what is possible through encouraging women into leadership roles. They also open doors and increase networks, so that a more diverse set of perspectives is available to the organization. Champions help to challenge the beliefs behind self-limiting behaviors and provide support and advice for the OTW. Champions, being proactive in the relationship, identify and promote new opportunities, encourage big stretches and make all the difference when the OTW hesitates.

Just do it!

When women spoke to us about being championed, they often mentioned being encouraged to acknowledge strengths and capabilities which they did not yet recognize. This was not about false admiration but about constructive support in challenging the OTW to reflect on how they needed to present their achievements for the next promotional opportunity.

The power of having your potential recognized by a well-respected senior leader is truly transformational. One of our respondents told us: "I was interested in an executive board level role and I thought that the CEO might be looking for minority candidates. Even so, I did not bring myself to the CEO's attention at this point. But he realized I would be interested – or maybe he thought I SHOULD be interested. Knowing my calibre and my experience, he initiated the conversation and, of course, I agreed to apply. The appointment committee saw me as the top qualified candidate and it all seemed to happen for me after that." Other cases in this book demonstrate similar examples, such as Tracy Clarke at Standard Chartered, who said no to her champion, Lord Davies, not once but twice! It is evident that when a senior leader acknowledges the latent ambition and ability of the OTW and encourages them to achieve these goals, the "barriers" are no longer an obstacle.

The impact of early championship

Very early championship from parents, other relatives, and family friends was a common theme but by no means universal. Having a supportive environment at home, with a variety of role models was key for some. The saying goes "it takes a village to raise a child." Well, it takes a cluster of close role models to raise a leader – parents, grandparents, and primary carers who believe that girls and boys should have equal opportunities to try things out and who encourage girls to be as ambitious and adventurous as boys; families who ask "what did you do today that you are proud of?"; families who are judicious in allocating challenging responsibilities and praise for hard work and achievement, rather than for obedience or "goodness."

One interviewee, a scientist who became a well-known Chair of a number of public-sector organizations, told us how her father expected the highest level of achievement from his daughters as well as his son, telling them, "You can do anything if you work hard enough."

Of course, not all our interviewees had that early championship. Others developed a robust sense of self-belief and responsibility for their own experiences and actions as a result of surviving difficult, even tragic, circumstances; for example, Dame Steve Shirley, one of our interviewees, who was a Kindertransport refugee in World War II. Building a strong sense of resilience is common amongst entrepreneurial leaders, and something we discuss in more detail in Chapter 8.

Teachers can be champions too. Rita Pierson's enthusiastic Ted Talk demonstrates the power of teachers as champions for children to build their confidence, even when the children doubt their own abilities. Many of our interviewees were given a fundamental base of confidence at school or university, because a teacher or head or lecturer believed passionately in gender equality and conveyed that to all the young people in their care, or because they specifically told girls and young women that they too were capable of anything, if they worked hard enough. There is of course a wider discussion to be had about schools and their responsibility in shaping expectations. Imagine the power of teacher training programs including unconscious bias awareness?

Championing throughout the career

Early championing is really powerful because it kick-starts the process of building confidence at an earlier stage. However, championing is incredibly powerful throughout a woman's career or business. We know building confidence is not always a linear process; women can get derailed through rejection, maternity leave, or other demands that conflict with their anticipated career path, as well as the normal setbacks any job entails.

Timing is critical, and to get the most out of championship, the relationship needs to start when the OTW is in the early stages of a new role, a career, or even a new business. It is estimated each of us will have seven career changes in our lifetime and with each change comes new challenges. Each new environment comes with the need to understand the dynamics, identify key players, and build strategic relationships with key decision-makers, all of which can be an outcome of the championing relationship.

Some of the women we interviewed described how the champions they met later on in their careers were instrumental in changing their trajectory. Joan Underwood, who is the Project Manager for the Caribbean Leadership Project and previously non-resident Ambassador for Antigua and Barbuda in several Latin American countries, describes how she met her champion after she completed her MBA. Her champion was Prime Minister Spencer, who identified her potential and scoped out a role for her in his office: "I had to leave a job in the private sector, with the income, perks, visibility to take up a public sector job. I resigned from my job. Friends and family asked me if I had lost my mind."

A head of the engineering department at a UK university described the impact of being championed further on in her career: "one of the critical points in my career (apart from being allowed time to do my PhD) was being picked out to work alongside one of the directors for 18 months. This gave me a whole new perspective on strategy and to have a view of the business at a globally corporate level."

The right champion or champions at the right stage in your life and career can be crucial, not only opening opportunities but encouraging you to take them up and coaching you to improve your chances of success. And it is most likely that women will need more than one champion, for different phases in their progress towards leadership, but also for different aspects of their activities. For example, a champion who is also a line manager can deliver confidence-boosting feedback and feedforward most effectively. Line managers can also help a woman articulate her own ambitions. But at the same time, a very senior champion can raise aspirations, provide more challenging opportunities that open up wider, more strategic horizons, and be a more powerful advocate both within and across organizations. Sue Clayton in the UK clearly articulates why leaders will take on this role: "If a leader has two or three good people in their team they will encourage them, even if it's not formally stated as sponsorship. They will nurture them. I've done it in my teams, if people are good and you want to fast track them through."

The value of early responsibility and broadening experience

You will remember that one common factor in the stories of our most successful women was that they had been given significant responsibilities early on. This is echoed in the famous story told by Christine Lagarde, whose parents felt that, at four, she was perfectly capable of being home alone for the occasional evening looking after her younger siblings while they went out – and she discovered that, although she was scared, she could also manage what was thrown at her.[1] Hannah Kimuyu, a director at Greenlight Digital in the UK, recognized the impact of early-stage responsibility; sometimes that level of responsibility was unwelcome at the time, but appreciated later: "My mother was very smart, perhaps the smartest woman I knew growing up. She gave us a lot of freedom, but a lot of responsibility too … I guess that is where my need for autonomy comes from." Nurjehan Mawani C.M., Aga Khan Development Network Diplomatic (AKDN) Representative, for Afghanistan, shared her experiences of taking responsibility to help her fellow pupils whilst at school by organizing tutorials to support them, without taking the credit for the effort: "The ethic very much promoted in our community, it's about self-help and also helping others. I'm not unique, there were many others who were similar. I was very struck that you could make a difference and I would watch how you could make a difference by putting in that extra bit."

Women who take the opportunity to take responsibility early on in their careers, even if not in childhood, gain both confidence and authority. It allows them to practice a broad base of skills, gain deep knowledge, and build a wide range of perspectives. At a recent seminar hosted by the business magazine *Management Today*, in Birmingham, UK, Alice Webb, Director of BBC Children's, described how her career path had taken her across many different opportunities during her ten years at the BBC. She was clear about the importance of a varied career in the same way as a varied diet: "The impact of diversity allows you to build your skills-set but also to recognize what you need to do or can do at certain stages."

Why is early responsibility and breadth of experience so important for leadership? Why might champions be looking for those with these characteristics? There are a number of possible reasons, based on our new leadership model:

1. Leaders are more confident and better able to manage stress; this is learned behavior. Having a chance to perform in a range of different contexts over time builds confidence in one's ability to handle different challenges, as well as manage effectively through change. Resilience to stress can also be built up through gradual exposure to greater challenges. This is more likely to occur naturally when roles change and grow frequently. Exposure to difficult people and conflicting demands is also more likely to happen with a broader range of experiences.

2. Leaders need a range of expertise on strategy, inspiration, communication, the industry, and world affairs. In other words, they need to become experts in broader leadership issues, not just a narrow functional knowledge, such as IT or Marketing. A range of experiences can help develop that strategic view. Shadowing a senior director, or being seconded to a project they lead, can expose them to that broader perspective. That personal exposure through action is much better for skills development than say studying for an MBA, though that helps develop the theoretical framework for the experience.

3. Leaders need the ability both to focus intensely and to change their focus rapidly. Changing circumstances and roles enable a great deal of practice in doing both. If you regularly take on not only new knowledge but a whole new set of unspoken assumptions and thinking

frameworks, then you need to be able to focus hard on learning, hearing, and paying attention to meaning and actions, not just words. And if you are working across a range of teams and disciplines, you need to learn to change your focus as something completely different acquires salience, urgency, and importance, compared to the day before.

4. Leaders need to be able to make good decisions. Exposure to diversity of experience and people helps combat stereotypes, confirmation bias, and proximity bias. Getting used to the way a number of different people or teams work to reach decisions can give you additional strategies for the future. Moving on means that you get used to focusing on the future rather than re-hashing the past.

Increasing confidence

If women's brains focus more on negative feedback, and their neurochemistry predisposes them to greater anxiety and lower levels of confidence than men, what can champions do later in life to help increase their confidence?

Although the link of confidence with testosterone is significant, it is possible for women to increase their confidence and even, according to some, their levels of testosterone and hence their confidence. Stretch assignments and roles with management responsibility help build experience, expertise, and trust, enabling you to solve problems, whatever they may be, with the right resources around you.

One important way of increasing confidence – and testosterone – is by succeeding: trying out a challenging task and doing well, and then trying another one which is slightly more stretching, and so on, builds confidence over time – and "winning" boosts testosterone levels. So engaging in challenging, competitive activities at the right level can be helpful, providing you win more often than you lose!

Earlier, we discussed the importance of increasing the level of challenge and responsibility of activities and succeeding in them. As a result, this underpins the development of confidence. The main role of champions in a work context might be seen as:

- Opening doors to opportunities over time and encouraging their OTW to take them up.
- Providing preparation advice and coaching so as to increase their chances of success and learning from failures rather than ruminating over them.
- Providing feedback and feedforward that can counteract self-doubt, imposter syndrome, and any tendency to deny due "ownership" of successes.

The fact that women are more sensitive to their social environment and the opinion of others might indicate that a champion, or champions, can be very influential at any stage of a woman's career, more so indeed than for men. A champion's recognition of potential, and desire to see it stretched and fulfilled, is an external affirmation of value, a declaration of belief in a woman's competence that, coming as it does from a respected senior leader, can contribute to developing self-belief.

Women can also increase their own confidence, according to Amy J. Cuddy and colleagues, by changing physical behavior.[2] Standing tall, with open shoulders, arms held high and chin lifted is the classic pose assumed by athletes after winning a race or a match, even if they are blind and haven't ever seen anyone do this. Two minutes of this pose is said to be enough to raise testosterone levels and lower cortisol levels, for about 20 minutes … and that increases the chances of a win in a difficult conversation or negotiation that follows. There was a challenge to these results by Eva Ranehill and her team in 2015, who argued that the actual differences in hormonal levels was insignificant or non-existent, but that confidence was still influenced by the person's own perception of the pose as denoting power.[3]

The opposite behavior to the power pose – sitting in a submissive pose, taking up as little space as possible, scrunched up with lowered eyes and chin – has the opposite effect. It lowers testosterone and increases cortisol levels, which indicate increased stress. And how often have you seen women sit like that in meetings, especially when they are in the minority?

Champions can give really effective personal feedback about matters such as stance, presence, style, and their impact that other people, even good friends, might shy away from. They can reflect how others see you. For example, Kitty remembers Bob, her line manager, a champion early in her career, who spent a lot of his time helping her gain the necessary skills for her promotion. The range of support varied from helping her to use new software to preparing concise but persuasive reports and managing feedback. Bob was the person who warned her that her manner occasionally seemed intimidating. Although Kitty found it painful and hard to believe, Bob offered her presentation skills training that helped improve her communication skills and taught her how to manage eye contact appropriately. He also showed her how her passion to get results quickly could be better channeled, so that people felt motivated not steamrollered. She learned to tailor her style appropriately to her audience and is still grateful for that feedback 30 years later.

A champion's commitment to, and belief in, their OTW, their interest in building their long-term confidence, and wanting them to succeed and be happy means they will have high expectations. They will be tough but fair in their demands, and considerate in the way they express them. In essence they are willing to put their "political capital" on the line for the OTW. Champions can become the opposite of the critical voice heard in the worst moments of imposter syndrome. They become the voice of your best self, the voice telling you that you can surpass your expectations. In fact the best champions give feedforward,[4] not comments or criticism about the past, but positive advice on how to do better in future.

This is where the additional characteristics of championship make a profound difference. A sponsorship relationship might not offer the kind of external belief that breeds self-belief. If your success is based on your usefulness to someone else, that becomes an external measure, rather than an internal one. Knowledge that you are useful, even essential, to the success of someone senior and more powerful is not quite the same as the knowledge that you can achieve what *you* set out to do, *you* can succeed, in a way that *you* determine and to criteria that *you* set, that *you* are the prime agent in shaping *your* life.

The role of organizations

Organizations that support championing do reap the benefits of additional confidence and ambition amongst women. They are less likely to lose able women at key career stress points, such as returning from maternity leave. Supporting championship at organizational level means increasing awareness of championing. It can also mean including awareness and training around championship as part of diversity and inclusion (D&I) initiatives. Encouraging championship at all levels and allowing for some flexibility so that a champion's voice as well as a line manager's can be heard when discussing talent identification, promotion, and training and development opportunities can all be powerful mechanisms for promoting women's progress. In most companies only line managers are specifically asked to suggest suitable candidates for so-called "high potential" development programs.

There are also some very practical processes that can help encourage championing. First, increasing opportunities for interactions between staff at senior and junior levels, so that talent identification and nurturing becomes a part of "the way we do things around here" openly. Other processes to support championship include building the recruitment and promotion of female staff into annual assessments of mid to senior line managers, a practice exemplified successfully for Royal Bank of Canada.[5] Over time, this has the potential to build a strong internal leadership culture that can also feed through internal training. Another mechanism that was used effectively for both men and women by the French company that was Thomson CSF (subsequently Thales) was to require the most senior managers to spend time as tutors at their corporate university (the fact that it was in a beautiful chateau outside Paris helped!). This helped forge some strong and long-term cross-company relationships.

Arun Jain, Director of Fluor Engineering in India, is very clear about the benefits of implementing a successful diversity policy:

> This didn't just occur; we made moves to instal women. These women act as role models for other women. We brought women in on new positions: one woman was planned for, the others it was working with them: one women refused but we didn't give up on her and approached her thrice before she agreed. These women acted as role models for other women. These women were groundbreaking because there was no prior experience of this, so there was a lot of fear and lack of role models. Once these women became leaders we worked with them on their confidence, leadership presence, and presentation skills, improved their ability to network laterally and with more senior leaders in the company.

Overcoming bias

Bias is notoriously hard to counteract, it is innate, intuitive, and often below consciousness. At individual level, simply being aware that it exists in ourselves is the first step. Pressing pause after an instinctive reaction to another person and challenging one's self is a useful discipline. Learning to reflect and challenge intuitive attitudes, reactions, and decisions and remembering most decisions are made subconsciously and then post-hoc consciously rationalized also helps. Women resent being stereotyped but then find they too may be labeling others – women and men – according to culturally defined expectations. Keep reminding yourself that equality does not mean being the same and that you need to respect, recognize, and allow for differences that are not defined by any gender, ethnicity, or other stereotypes. Barbara Judge, the first female Chair of the UK's Institute of Directors describes the impact of bias on aspirations of school children who will still assign gender stereotypes to certain careers: "Ask a group of schoolgirls to close their eyes and picture a surgeon, a chief executive, or a pilot. Then ask those who visualized a woman to raise their hands: only one or two will go up, if any."[6] Hold in mind examples of people who surprised you by not being at all what you expected. Challenge your opinion of yourself, not just others. Learning to tune in to this level of self-awareness and challenging yourself will not happen overnight. It needs motivation and constant practice – and can be hugely helped by a challenging champion or coach.

Combating bias at organizational level also depends on raising awareness and acceptance that it is real and shared; it is about "all of us," not just "them." Having processes to ensure diversity in decision-making groups, especially when hiring, promotions, and development are at stake, as we said above, can be very effective. Having protocols that elicit both intuitive responses and rational assessment of evidence can also help. For example, a form for job applications that includes scoring against pre-set objective criteria for both job requirements and personal specification, as well as a question about feelings, or one that only puts any personal information (that might give hints as to gender) at the end, might be helpful.

Leadership from the top does set the tone, exemplified by the companies in our case studies – for example, Fluor in India. A diverse board and senior executive team can provide everyday role models that challenge bias. Public commitment from senior leadership is a serious attractor to encourage action on gender diversity.

Overcoming self-limitation and hesitation

In our early research we found that women acknowledged that to some extent they were responsible for holding themselves back. And later, when we conducted our international research, we saw that confirmed, both by women who were being championed and their champions. In some cases, this self-limitation was due to a lack of confidence. For many women, it was a champion who encouraged them and gave them the confidence to step up to a career challenge. Kate Reid, in New Zealand, says, "I had a wonderful woman boss – she had a very clear view … (one of the) inspirational people who helped me figure out what I wanted to do and gave me confidence."

Sometimes, this self-limitation was due to conflicting goals between spending time with the family and working. A woman we spoke to was conscious that staying for too long with her public sector employer, because she felt that it was a safe and tolerant environment for working mothers, might have limited her career options. "I have been in the same department all my life. A lot of people move around a lot. I did have a varied career. It raised questions amongst recruiters but it was safer to stay in the same department because I had time off with children."

Some described how their expectations had been lowered: they had been discouraged from being ambitious, from seeing themselves as having great potential, or they had been categorized as not quite good enough for some next step at some point in their lives. Many women rise to that as a challenge and are determined to prove these judgments wrong, but others internalize them and live down to the expectations. In the last 15 years or so, the fact that the brain is plastic – that is, changeable – in adults has become widely known and accepted. But we still pigeonhole children and young people into categories as though their abilities could not be developed throughout their lives; this one is "academic," that one isn't, and that one will never achieve anything. We have only recently realized the extent to which determination, motivation, focused attention, and practice can enable amazing achievements and development of capabilities. Of course, limitations and differences in natural capacity exist and matter, but our point is that most people can and do improve if given the encouragement, self-belief, and the opportunity to learn and practice that championship offers.

One characteristic of the champions we have spoken to is that they truly believe those they champion can change and improve and surpass their own highest expectations. That external affirmation can be a very powerful driver for women. It can help them overcome their own biases and learn how to deal with those of others. If someone you admire and respect denies the validity of a self-limiting belief, helps you by pointing out your own evidence that contradicts a biased stereotype, then you might start to question your thinking.

Saying no to opportunity

Champions can be hugely influential when women hesitate, then choose to turn down an opportunity for reasons that are more to do with lack of confidence than lack of ability. They become skilled at handling knockbacks when their high potential OTW says no to a daunting new role. The champion pushes back, firmly. They have invested in encouraging this person and this can include pushing them beyond their comfort zone. The impact of championship is most potent during stress points experienced by women, especially during the early stages of their careers where they feel uncertain about their aspirations, or on returning from maternity leave.

Attributing your success to luck and others' to merit and their own actions

Champions help challenge the beliefs behind these behaviors. When women spoke to us about being championed they often mentioned being encouraged to acknowledge strengths and capabilities which they did not yet recognize, achievements which they did not feel they owned. Champions had helped them to think through how to recognize and present their achievements in preparation for the next role and the one after that. A champion may point out areas which need working on but will mostly focus on strengths.

A good champion will keep up to date with your progress and ask questions which elicit your achievements. That kind of conversation, in an atmosphere of trust, in itself can remind you of what you have done and help you recalibrate how you compare yourself with your peers. A champion will also have a good sense of when you should be thinking of a move and how best to make that move. By virtue of their seniority and greater experience they will also be able to help you understand and navigate the system or systems for promotion in a way that helps you see that you have to take responsibility for making that next step in your career.

Perhaps best of all, a champion can show you that you are not only allowed to take pride and pleasure in your achievements, you are required to do so. That attributing others' success to merit and your own to luck is not modesty but a refusal to take responsibility for your own job and career, for yourself. A champion can do that from a perspective of wanting what is best for you. The beauty of championship is that in such circumstances, doing what is best for you is also more likely to lead to what is best for the organization, as you are more likely to be more able as well as motivated to perform. It is not about being selfish, about distorting the organization's interests to suit your own, but about being properly responsible and accountable and playing your full part in the process of your performance as well as your career progression; not leaving it to luck or other people, or blaming others if it didn't work out. It is about being assertive enough to value your own contribution appropriately, to ask for the additional resources you need in order to do the job really well, rather than feel you are not worth that additional investment, or that luck means someone will spot you are nearing burn-out. It is also about seeing yourself as valuable in your own right, not just in terms of whether you are being helpful to others or sacrificing your own chance of a good performance for some unspecified other requirement.

Tasks

For individuals:

Think about anyone who has been a champion for you.

Note down your responses to the following questions:

- What did they do?
- Why was their support important to you?
- What was the impact of their support?

Think about the next few roles where you are stepping up into more senior positions. Try and imagine you are the head of your organization as you answer the following questions:

- What do you think would keep you awake at night?
- What strategic changes do you think you would need to consider?

- How has your perspective changed?
- Who can you call on for advice?

For organizations:

- What examples of championing already exist in your organization – formally and informally?
- What do you need to build a championing environment in your organization?
- What stories of championing success can you build within your organization or across your sector?

5 {.chapter-number}

chapter

Getting Ready for Championship

A new chapter in Maya's career has opened. She is thriving in a great but demanding job, she is well-known across the company. Her champion, Dara, is supportive, but too busy to be closely involved in Maya's career development. Maya is still learning, not just about the technical aspects of her role, but especially about how to lead people when they do not report directly to you. She finds she is really good at this aspect of her work, and enjoys getting people from a wide range of organizations, across many continents and cultures, to pull together towards a common goal. Having seen how much she is enjoying her new role, and realizing that without Dara's support she would have missed this experience and growth, she ponders on what she needs to do to make sure that next time she is ready.

Laying the foundations

The key to success is to find the right champion (or champions) for each phase of your career and to know how to utilize the relationships effectively. As we have already said, the most effective champions are individuals who are senior leaders and able to identify and provide opportunities to further your career. These individuals are incredibly busy and so will invest their time and resources sparingly. It is therefore imperative that you spend time preparing for the championing relationship. In this chapter, we show you how to prepare yourself so that you can reap the benefits of championship. Ambition is a big part of this – knowing what you want to achieve, even if you are not sure how you want to get there, is an important part of this process.

There is no one standard approach to championing. The experiences of the women and men we spoke to demonstrated a wide range of relationships, both in terms of how they developed and continued. As discussed in the previous chapter, championship is not a one-hit approach and whilst it can be very powerful in the earlier stages of a career, we have also witnessed its impact throughout the process of building a career. In every case in our interviews, the championing relationship was initiated by the champion who recognized the potential of the "one to watch" (OTW) and identified the value they could add by championing, as illustrated by the case of Maria Msiska in Kenya: "The bosses I've worked for have been great mentors and have given me a lot of support with my work. They have helped me to climb the career ladder."

When we looked carefully at our data, however, we noticed that successful female leaders did not sit back and wait to be noticed. Even women in the earlier stages in their careers demonstrated small but important proactive approaches as their responsibilities grew. They were curious and eager for new and stretching opportunities. They recognized that taking responsibility for projects that were hard was good experience and that it also raised their profile. They actively sought out responsibility and welcomed accountability. And they realized that in taking responsibility for their own career progression they had to take some risks, they had to take up new opportunities and owning their successes was essential. Jude Kelly, UK, embodies this spirit in her views: "I was the kind of person who tried to do things, got things done, wasn't going to take no for an answer, all of that."

Actively seeking out opportunities to take on more responsibility is a great way of demonstrating that you have the (spare) capacity to grow and also bringing yourself to the attention of potential champions. And what does "looking out for new opportunities" mean in practice? It means being curious and open: asking questions and having conversations about what others are doing around you. It means paying attention to what is happening in your industry or sector, keeping up to date through news, trade, and social media. It might mean asking to attend a relevant conference or putting yourself on the mailing list for the proceedings. It could mean having lunch in the canteen with a different group of people every day. It is focusing on the positive, on what you can gain from where you are and what you are doing, however difficult your situation, that enables you to learn as much as possible. Sabrina Dar, Kenya, says:

> I was enrolled in a two year program of rotation every six months. I got used to being a new girl, with no access to resources and I realized I had to do things quickly to make an impact. That never left me. I have never stayed anywhere for longer than two years. I continued that learning for five years, became the most junior analyst reporting to the most senior. I didn't always "sit at the table" but I didn't mind that as I was learning about seniors and developing teams. I then took a role in Strategy at EMEA where I worked with an external consultant who had just been brought in-house. It was just a small team and I learned a completely different way of thinking.

Taking control: responsibility, values, and goals

In the first few years, not having a career plan is the norm for the majority of women – and quite a few men as well. This is a time when having a broad range of experiences is crucial, both within one organization or across many. This is when early championship has proved to be so valuable, where a senior is able to have enough knowledge of the work of a junior to appreciate their talent and want to help them develop their potential. Furthermore, even if the OTW does not know their plans, the champion can provide the opportunity to lift their line of vision higher and map out a more strategic perspective. Almost all of the women we interviewed who made it to the top had that experience, although they used different language to describe it.

Sandi Beattie, New Zealand, claims: "When I lived in Auckland, I knew Helen (Clark, later PM) as an MP and I was a member of the Labour Party and she needed someone to work in her office. She was very supportive; she wanted capable people working for her and she was interested in capable women. This was a fantastic experience; working in parliament gives you a clear, unique insight into the workings of government, and working for a Minister was a great experience."

Our previous research in 2011 had revealed that, for the majority of women, early talent spotting is the exception rather than the rule. We have spoken to many women who felt that, in their early years, they were invisible to senior managers, in spite of their talent and a growing track record of success. They seemed to be stuck on a very sticky ground floor. Those women who managed to come unstuck with a champion progressed very quickly and, looking back, said they wished they had been more assertive about their career aspirations earlier on. They saw the need to have acknowledged their ambition and developed goals to help channel their motivation.

One extremely able woman described how things became much clearer to her when she moved from the public sector to a senior frontline "hard" managerial role in a multinational bank. She had not realized what she was *not* doing until she saw the way the younger, more junior, men around her in her new job were behaving. The men were finding ways, subtle and not so subtle, to bring themselves to the attention of their seniors, not just to her as their line manager, but to her boss and to leaders two or three levels up. The men "bumped into" the senior staff in the corridor or on the "smoking step," and said a few words about how well their current project was going and how good it was for the bank. The men dropped into a senior's office to ask if there was any information they could provide for the next exec team meeting. One junior male employee even told her that he wanted HER job in a couple of years' time!

Many women would describe that kind of behavior as pushy and inauthentic. As we discussed in Chapter 3, women who push are judged more harshly than men, by both men and women.[1] For the men in this story, this type of behavior was perfectly acceptable, but imagine retelling this story with the genders swapped. The reactions to women declaring their ambitions and door-stepping senior managers would be most likely very negative.

Women find they are precariously balancing the need to be explicit about ambition and demonstrate credibility without attracting negative perceptions. It is very hard for women to get that balance right. Indeed, there are women who push too hard and create strong reactions. One senior female executive in the UK finance industry claimed: "There are women who go about it the wrong way, they try too hard and they push too artificially. I want to tell them not to be so desperate, to be patient. Sometimes women overcompensate for lack of confidence."

So what can women do to put themselves in a position where they will be ready to reap the benefits of championship when they are recognized as having high potential? The answer lies in preparing yourself to communicate your vision powerfully, own your career and demonstrate your achievements to build your confidence, and challenge the biases that we know create hesitation.

Take more responsibility for the direction of your career

Taking more responsibility for your own career is key. It shows others that you are capable of acting independently. Champions are busy people and are not looking for dependents. Champions do not see themselves as a permanent support function for your career. They see themselves as a point of leverage, aiming for where they can achieve the greatest impact. They are looking for those with talent, who having been given opportunities can take them, make best use of them, and even eventually pass them on effectively to others. True champions don't want to "own" you or your career.

Taking ownership of your own career starts with assuming that it is your responsibility and that, if you are stuck, it is up to you to do something about it. That takes confidence and courage. In Chapter 4, we spoke about how to increase confidence, and increased confidence can lead to courage. Ownership doesn't mean having your career all mapped out, but it is important to have a clear idea of the scope of your ambition. Even if your trajectory is not precise, do you feel you know enough about your aspirations to give yourself a direction, at least for the next few years?

We are not saying you have to have a clearly defined career plan; in fact very few of the women we interviewed had anything like a career plan when they set off to work for the first time. A few clearly knew what sector they wanted to work in; whether it was law or engineering, politics, teaching or social work, or running a restaurant. In most of these cases their first steps were shaped by advice from peers, but what was interesting was how many of them had a strong sense of purpose, of values, a sense of the kinds of things they wanted to explore, and the curiosity to try new things out. In one example Jan Owen, who created the world's largest social enterprise, describes how her passion determined her choices: "I went back to where my heart was (working with young people), having worked with corporates and refugees. I was always looking for entrepreneurial ways of doing things." One academic in the UK claimed: "Starting from what might look like the beginning, I went to Cambridge thinking I was a physicist and discovered materials and metallurgy. My attraction was partly aesthetic – the beauty of the images – and partly the relationship between fun and serious study." For Robyn Joy Pratt, her grandmother provided a huge influence: "I always aspired to be like my grandmother, she always pushed to do the best she could for others. I always look to the development of the team. I was more inspired by her actions than by her life." So if you don't know exactly what you want to do, where you want to get to, and what you want to achieve as a result, how can you start to set a direction for yourself?

Know your values

Identifying your values helps you understand what drives your behaviors and might help give you a sense of purpose and direction; even an idea of what you want your legacy to be. We know values are the essential meaning that the emotions assign to the inputs that come through our senses. The eight basic emotions are like a spectrum, on a range from fear to love, and they tell us whether something is to be avoided ("bad") or approached ("good"), whether it is undesirable or desirable.[2] Our feelings, states, and moods are like the myriad of colors and shades that can be created from combinations of those eight basic emotions. Of course, our values are more complex and difficult to analyze. They are the result of our cultures, environments, and the evolution of our human nature. They are conscious or unconscious drivers of our behaviors. It is important for anyone to understand what drives their behaviors, but especially important for leaders, as their behaviors drive those of so many others.

When we speak about values we tend to use the word to denote only those values which we deem to be positive, to which we are attracted; those values which we deem to be "good." Such values are attractors, lodestones of our behaviors. Values can be linked to the even more powerful escape/avoidance/survival emotions. For example, survival is something of the greatest value. Perceived threats to survival are something we perceive as "bad," to be avoided almost at any cost. Any perceived threat to survival does not need to be physical, or even real, in order to trigger very strong responses. The same circuits are activated in the brain by social threats, such as fear of dismissal, as when we fear our lives might be in danger – say, seeing a dark shadow below a triangular fin when swimming in the sea.

Social threats can be of different types. At work, for example, a perceived threat to the security of our job, to our authority, or status can be very frightening. Public humiliation leading to reputational damage and shame are very real threats. Fear is a limiting emotion, because it focuses the resources of our brain very narrowly onto the cause of the fear and on the simplest and quickest way to escape from the threat. This narrow focus restricts our ability to make the kind of connections that might lead to a creative solution or mitigation of the threat. There has been a great deal of work examining the connections between stress and inhibited creativity, as demonstrated by Robert Epstein in his book, *The Big Book of Creativity Games.*[3]

Clarifying your values is important because they drive your behavior, whether you are aware of them or not. There may be values which remain below your level of consciousness, but as far as possible try to surface what your values really are. In order to clarify your values, you need to articulate them, describing them to yourself and others, and writing them down helps as well. What question might you ask yourself? How do I want to be remembered? What gives me the most pleasure in life? Do I work in order to fulfill my potential, find out what I am capable of achieving? How do I count my success? What am I most afraid of in my life?

Understanding your values is not a once in a lifetime activity. It is an iterative process where you get used to questioning yourself in relationship to what you are doing. Having a clearer sense of your values enables you to live with purpose and this begins to focus the energy you need to invest in decision-making. Furthermore, when we work for a purpose and our actions are aligned to our values we have more energy and momentum to achieve our goals, even if we have not yet fully defined them.

Living a life with purpose means living a fulfilled life and this is necessary to inspire others to champion you and to follow you. In the words of Albert Einstein: "Nothing truly valuable arises from ambition or from a mere sense of duty; it stems rather from love and devotion towards men (and women) and towards objective things."[4] Having a sense of purpose, recognizing your desire to achieve, your ambition, is like setting your compass.

Goals and why they matter

Why are goals so important? Why do we put such emphasis on setting goals? Goals encapsulate what you want to achieve. Articulating your goals and indeed writing them down, makes it more likely that you will succeed in those achievements. Goals enable you to make your dreams a reality, turn your vision into the true story of your life.

It sounds so simple, but of course it isn't. We know that most human actions are goal driven. Think about the following actions; I pick up a biscuit because I am hungry, walk upstairs to find my keys, turn my head to hear better, pay attention to a noise to ascertain whether it represents a threat. Like values, goals can be both conscious and sub-conscious. The human brain is geared towards enabling goal driven actions, whether that is picking up a glass and filling it so that I might drink, or giving feedback with a low, gentle, friendly voice and a smile, because I want the feedback to be heard positively.

Goals, whether conscious or sub-conscious, help focus our attention, so that setting conscious goals is a way of ensuring that we help direct our mind and actions towards a desired outcome, and away from distractions, thus increasing the chances of success.

Figure 5.1 identifies the seven steps necessary to set better goals, by which we mean goals that are easier to achieve. Some of these will already be familiar but others may need a little more discussion.

When setting goals there are a number of questions you need to ask yourself:

1. Are my goals co-ordinated between the short, medium, and long term.
2. Are my goals specific and clear, so that I and others will know when they are achieved?
3. Are my goals measurable and time bound in terms of achieving something specific? Will I know whether I have achieved them or not, by a set date?
4. Do my goals reflect what is within my control?
5. When my goals are written down, how do I feel about them and who can I share them with to help me to be accountable for my plans?
6. Do my goals provide an opportunity for me to realistically stretch from my current position?
7. Are my goals consistent with my values?

FIGURE 5.1 Seven steps for setting better goals

Source: © Shaheena Janjuha Jivraj, 2014.

Running through these questions and developing greater clarity on your goals and how they are developed will help you to define them more clearly. They also build a sense of a contract with yourself and others, which we know increases motivation. Sharing goals that are clear, aligned, and have a solid foundation can help you to build a strong relationship with your champion – quite apart from the fact that if you do not know your real goals, no one else will. Without a clear idea of where you are going, you will not be able to access the support to get to where you want to be.

What are the advantages in being open about your goals? Discussing and testing them with a champion provides you with crucial feedback from someone with a broader and more experienced strategic vision. Trusting the champion with your goals builds a closer relationship and enables the champion to become more committed to your ambitions by being part of your plan.

Goals act as reference points; if you set something as a goal it is more satisfying to achieve it than if you had reached the same result without the goal. The same principle applies in reverse, so that not achieving a

Getting Ready for Championship   85

goal leads to greater dissatisfaction than if a goal had not been set. "One recipe for a dissatisfied adulthood is setting goals that are especially diffi-cult to attain," observes Daniel Kahneman, in his book, *Thinking, Fast and Slow*. He goes on to explain how goals impact our sense of well-being: "The goals that people set for themselves are so important to what they do and how they feel about it that an exclusive focus on experienced well-being is not tenable. We cannot hold a concept of well-being that ignores what people want."[5]

Baumeister said that the first step in self-control is setting a goal.[6] This acts as a set point around which we can regulate emotions and behaviors. In other words, without knowing what we want to achieve we cannot manage our own behaviors; we cannot truly own and be responsible for our careers.

Dangers of conflicting goals

For our goals to work for us they need to be aligned with our values. For example, we often say integrity is a key leadership characteristic. Integrity can be defined as honesty or truthfulness, but it is more than that, it is the consistency and coherence between emotions, thoughts, values, words, and actions. Integrity does not mean rigidity, or avoid-ing change. A leader with integrity can change and will do their best to explain why. We know that people can pick up a lack of consistency between words and actions, or even between oral and body language. Over time, people will notice a lack of coherence in someone who *says* their people are their greatest asset, but never seems to listen to what their people say. Conflicting signals breed mistrust. If our goals are signifi-cantly conflicting between themselves or with our values, people around us will pick this up.

Conflicting goals breed unhappiness in ourselves too. Everyone has goals that are likely to conflict at times – for example, family, leisure, and work goals. If we only set conscious goals for our work, then what we want to achieve for our family and our own self-actualization can get driven by sub-conscious goals and compromised by the greater clarity of our work goals. If our values embrace both our personal and work lives, then our conscious goals must follow.

Conflicting goals result in:

- Worry – the more competing demands you face, the more time you spend thinking about them.
- Lower productivity – you get less done, replacing action with rumination.
- Stress – your health suffers, physically and mentally. People with conflicting goals reported more anxiety, complaints, and visits to doctors.

Resolving the conflicts

If conflicting goals are inevitable, then how do you maintain your integrity without compromising on getting results? One way of navigating this dilemma is to set long-, medium-, and short-term goals. The long-term, high-level "life" goals are explicitly aligned with your core values. They help define priorities. For example, if I strive to be a good leader at work and a good mother at home, the best I can be, rather than perfect, that allows me to balance my priorities. My measures are what I achieve at work, the happiness and fulfillment of my children, and that my family and my colleagues will speak of me with affection and respect. Once an overarching longer-term goal is in place, then medium- and short-term goals can be set so as to be compatible with the parameters of your long-term goals. We know achieving goals takes self-discipline and energy, and so it is essential not to have too many goals at each stage.

Setting longer-term goals is good for you. It helps to focus your attention on a longer time horizon, within which it is possible to envisage a range of positive sub-goals. So perhaps the most effective strategy might be to set overarching goals aligned to core values, sufficiently specific so that their achievement is measurable – in some way. If these are set thoughtfully, realistically, and frequently revisited, adjusted and then rehearsed, then they become embedded and can act as the lodestone to your compass, focusing attention on opportunities to achieve them when these arise.

Setting medium-term goals that are more specifically delineated, and within these short-term goals that are action oriented (such as a short daily or weekly to do list), will then enable focus on what is needed but provide flexibility to change if meeting medium- or short-term goals threatens the achievement of the longer-term goals.

Short-term goals provide benefits of being like stepping stones and the positive reinforcement of having achieved smaller goals that can help to build confidence and a sense of competence or self-efficacy.[7] Being able to see the relationship between the short term and the long term will help you to handle the more difficult or boring aspects of a job that need to be done every day to achieve success over the longer term; such as foregoing immediate pleasure for longer-term gain – for example, finishing that project report rather than going out with a friend after work.

Pursuing our goals successfully is dependent both on focus (the ability to keep information active in working memory) and flexibility (the ability to change that focus and information when required). Attention is responsible for maintaining a balance between focus and flexibility, and there is evidence that attention levels do not always have to have reached consciousness in order to maintain that balance. Focusing attention on what is consciously willed or intended has the additional benefit of taking attention and energy AWAY from perhaps less desirable unconscious goals.

Organizations can help in the process by including career planning as part of the regular process of performance review by line managers. How often in your career reviews are you asked what your short-, medium-, and even longer-term goals are? Or when you are asked these questions, how often do you stop and really think about what they are and what they mean to you right now? We find more often than not when we ask women these questions that they haven't really stopped to think about what their own aspirations might be and need not only to be asked, but encouraged to spend some time thinking about it. If companies want to keep their talented women, they need to support them in thinking about their futures. Without some encouragement to discuss their longer-term goals and ambitions, women do not often consider how they might operate in the future in their working environment.

Returning from maternity leave is a transition period which can be immensely disruptive both at home and at work. It is a time when many companies find there is considerable turnover of staff. The reasons most often cited for non-returners after maternity leave focus on practical aspects such as childcare, affordability, and flexibility.[8] There are also deeper reasons: maternity leave can be a catalyst for women to reconsider their values and goals in relation to their career and work environments, and if there is conflict it makes it easier for women to consider leaving.

Organizations can help women to become more conscious and explicit about their goals; for example, some women's networks, internal and external, provide opportunities for women to expand their experiences, find new role models and test out their ambitions with peers in a safe environment. Organizations can offer other initiatives to encourage women to share their ambitions. For example, where championing is an explicit part of the culture, women can be encouraged to seek advice from more senior managers.

Champions will open the door, but they do not define where you want to go and who you want to be

What happens if you are still unsure of your goals, or just feel you want a change but are not yet sure what that change might be? We have worked with a number of women who in mid-career suddenly realize that they are no longer learning in their current role; they are not being stretched, but they don't really know what they want to do next, other than it must be different to what they are doing now. They become restless and dissatisfied and seek advice from friends, contacts, colleagues, mentors, coaches, and family, but their next step still doesn't seem to gel. They might ask their champion or champions, and get some great ideas and advice. However, the champion can only lay out options in relation to what the woman is consciously considering. It is not a champion's job to tell you what or who you want to be, nor are they fortunetellers to predict your future options.

Tasks

For individuals:

Earlier in the CHAMP model, we asked you to think about what your big picture would look like. This is a chance to start molding it.

Where do you see yourself in five years' time? Use the questions below to stimulate your thinking. Use action words rather than titles or roles. For example, use "develop and manage the implementation of a financial strategy that will underpin success for my company," rather than "Finance Director."

Once you have identified your big picture, use the mind map (Figure 5.2) to determine what the enablers and inhibitors are. As you identify the inhibitors, think about what you need in order to address the barriers they present. Find a trusted friend or family member to talk through with you what you have jotted down and help you reflect on what it means.

For individuals and organizations:

Try to set some goals that reflect your big picture ambitions. You can start wherever you feel comfortable, but try at least one or two long-term goals, perhaps two medium-term ones, and no more than three or four short-term goals. How you define the timescale is up to you. Using the table below (based on the goals wheel in Figure 5.1), fill in each section to help shape your goals.

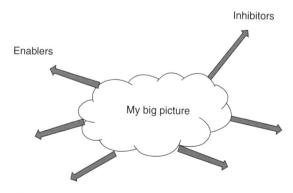

FIGURE 5.2 / **Sample mind map**

How will I measure success? What measures and timeframes do I need to ensure I know I have achieved my goal?

How can I make my goals specific; simple and clear, so that I and others will know when they are achieved?

How do I feel about my goals when they are written down and who can I share them with to help me to be accountable for my plans?

How are my goals consistent with my values?

How do my goals reflect what is within my control?

How do my goals provide an opportunity to realistically stretch from my current position?

How are my goals co-ordinated between the short, medium, and long term?

6

chapter

Developing the Championing Relationship

Maya launched into her new role with determination. The pressure of being in a new environment and feeling the need to make her mark has taken its toll. Nine months in and she is working all hours to stay on top of her job. Her son is being bullied at school. Maya feels guilty because she feels she is not giving him the right level of support. Naturally, her colleagues pick up on her anxiety and some rumors are circulating to the effect that she may be overstretched. These concerns reach the ears of her champion who had assumed all was going well. She asks Maya over for a coffee to check in with her and give her a heads-up. Her champion has taken the time to help her be more aware of how she is impacting on her team and on their perception of her, which could either make or break her in this new role. Maya is advised to take some time to sort things out at home, to prioritize her workload ruthlessly, to smile and assume a positive stance, to act as though she is not only on top of this job, but more than ready for her next promotion.

Communication, negotiation, trust, and fairness

So you've been identified as someone with potential. Perhaps, like a few of our interviewees, you have been asked to take on a very difficult change management role that crosses all the organizational boundaries, or you have been sent on a leadership development program. Perhaps like some others, you have been asked to take on a secondment, internal or external; to manage a difficult project with tough timescales, resource problems, and warring stakeholders. And maybe you said no to start off with … you were not sure you could do it really well, but were persuaded you had the right combination of skills and persistence and finally agreed.

Now what? How do you continue that conversation with the person who helped you find that challenge and discover that you were up to it? How do you develop that relationship? Do you develop that relationship? Or do you say thank you … and then move on?

Building a championing relationship relies on several drivers; clear ambitions and goals and strong motivation on the one hand and a powerful desire to see talent developed and utilized fully on the other. We have touched on these in the preceding chapters and in this chapter we will build on those principles to help you develop a clearer sense of what you can do to forge an effective relationship with your champion.

Communication

Communication is one of the most difficult aspects of successful leadership. Building a relationship with a champion can demand that you step out of your comfort zone, and require you to plan how to communicate with those who you want to recruit as trusted advisors and allies – most often under quite tight time pressures.

Understanding some of the fundamental rules of communication can be helpful in working out how to manage a successful championing relationship.

1. Do it!

The first rule in communication is do it, which means receiving as well as transmitting and ideally more of the former than the latter. What are the important questions YOU need to ask your champion in the early stages of the relationship? The list below gives you examples of the questions that are important for you to ask your champion:

- What do you as my champion hope I might achieve?
- What resources do I need for this role – are they available to me or can my champion help to get them?
- What sort of feedback do I need from my champion – when and how often?
- What updates do I need on the bigger picture in the organization/ sector?
- How can my champion help me to keep relevant people informed of my progress?
- Have I mapped out my network to see who else I need to communicate with about this role?

Some women find that taking time to keep communication going regularly with a champion is hard. It can seem like a distraction from their core purpose and their immediate goals, particularly when they are at full capacity with work and domestic demands. They feel they can do without yet another demand in their lives. But if you can see this level of commitment to a relationship as an additional investment, not just in your own career advancement, but in the resources you can eventually bring not only to your current project but the next one, the time appears to be well justified. A championship relationship is not a closed loop, but a way of being open to new ideas and new people too. Your champion, being more senior, is likely to communicate with different communities at different levels, and you will benefit from that.

Of course, your champion should not be your only route to conversations that open up broader horizons and expose you to new ideas and diverse perspectives.

Finally, when you can see the end of a short- to medium-term assignment, or you are looking for a substantial change, how do you find out what else might be available? Who do you ask? In whom do you confide your aspirations and career plans? If you have not kept these conversations going on a regular basis with your champion, your line manager, your wider networks, it gets harder to "go back." We have heard from many women how they are reluctant to initiate the discussion about their ambitions and aspirations with their line managers. They are concerned lest they appear to think too highly of themselves, or seem too demanding, or even pushy. They perceive that kind of discussion as difficult, even when their manager is asking about their ambitions. Often they tell us that they have no problem having exactly that kind of discussion on behalf of a deserving member of their staff, but find it impossible when it is about themselves. We found that preparing yourself, and rehearsing what you want to say and how you say it with your champion, means you are ready for that conversation with a manager, even if it happens unexpectedly.

Women often assume that if their champion or line manager has seen how well they are doing, they will know that they are ready for the next step, or even the one after that, and will do something about it! "Just do it" means speak up clearly about your aims and aspirations, what you want to achieve at every appropriate opportunity, communicate not just *what* you want to do next but that you are the kind of person who has the capacity to make a success of her next step – and not just with words, but with your demeanor, your stance, your smile, and appearance – as if you are already there. It makes it easier for people to see you in that next role.

2. Don't assume

Our second rule is **don't assume** – anything. Communication is really hard because the way my brain creates the world is not the way yours does, what I hear is not what you hear, and the same word has very different meanings for me than for you. Although our brains have evolved to support our social interactions, and the majority of human beings are quite good at interpreting others' intentions, human communication is far from perfect and we can get other people's meanings very wrong indeed. Our brains make sense of the world when there is inadequate information by filling in the gaps based on our previous experiences. We cannot help making assumptions, because filling in the blanks helps us navigate our environment successfully. Some scientists say that our brains are like "prediction machines," because they not only fill in the blanks but anticipate the future based on the past.[1] Understanding that these are our assumptions, that this is the way our brains work, rather than the objective reality, should give us pause for thought – literally.

So take the time to think about and check your understanding of what someone else means and do not be afraid of repeating what someone has said in your own words to make sure you have understood them properly. Remember too that you cannot assume common knowledge, that others' experiences and background will give them the same connotations around what some words or actions mean, or that you can know how someone will react to new knowledge. For example, don't assume that your champion knows you are having a great time because the project is such an interesting one. Think about how you convey your enthusiasm and gratitude when they have helped you. Don't assume that the resources that you so obviously will need will be made available to you automatically if you do not ask for them. And don't assume that you WON'T get what you ask for!

One senior female director we spoke to described how she realized she had to ask for what she wanted to take on the role, and how she had assumed that she would not be given what she asked for:

> Then there was an ongoing conversation. I kept saying no and he kept coming back. I had a meeting with a mentor and he said what would it take for you to take this job? I wanted a seat on the board, to report to the president not to a general manager, I wanted an executive coach, I wanted a budget and I wanted to hold people accountable. My mentor said why don't you ask for that? SO I thought maybe I should. We had a final meeting and I laid out my conditions, and then I leant back and thought I can gracefully step away. He paused for 20 seconds and said: OK I do need you to do this and if that's what you want, OK you can have them. So when do you start?

Assuming that someone else knows what you want is a trap that many women fall into. They quite often believe that their behavior is enough to signal intent, and if not, that dropping subtle hints will work. It is also true that *on average*, women tend to be more empathetic than men. But it is not true of all women, and many men are very empathetic and many women are not. Therefore no one – male or female – should assume that the person with whom they are communicating has the same level of empathy or understanding as they do – or think they do!

If the other person knows you extremely well, has empathetically heard what you mean, and they have your welfare as a primary concern, they will take the time and trouble to try and understand your ambitions, or at least ask you about them. The same may also be said for individuals for whom you are an important part of their future. But *you* need to take responsibility for being clear, explicit, and open about what you really want. Don't waste a champion's or manager's time by skirting round the issues and throwing out hints.

Some organizations are getting better at finding ways of eliciting career plans and embedding the practice of being open about them into their culture. For example, eBay has worked to create a more inclusive environment for their female employees.[2] One of the few rules they instigated as part of their strategy was that it is every line manager's responsibility to elicit the career ambitions of their female staff as an essential part of their annual appraisal. Setting that rule is a great idea. Making sure that line managers implement it effectively might need more effort, such as appropriate training.

3. Think before you speak

The third rule of communication is **think before you speak – most of the time**! If the conversation is planned, take a few moments to think about what you might want to achieve as a result, and try to imagine what the others may want from it that might differ from your purpose. Your purpose and how you achieve it will to some extent depend on the nature of your relationship with the other person. It can be quite simple, as with a friend; to enjoy the other person's company, or just to share some interesting news. Being too conscious about having a purpose can, of course, get in the way of a casual chat. The key is to be appropriate to the relationship. In a championship relationship, for example, where the champion is often much more senior and as such likely to have more pressure on their time, being focused on making the communication as effective and efficient as you can shows thoughtful respect. That doesn't mean you can't have some fun too!

How you present yourself and building the practice of thinking before you speak takes time and requires practice. It is not something that happens overnight. Exercises like practicing mindfulness can be a powerful way to help you build the discipline of slowing down before you speak. Think about the most powerful leaders in your organization, and how they pace their communication, how they balance their time between listening, thinking, and speaking. We often talk about strong leadership being associated with self-discipline and self-control, and this includes how we communicate.[3]

Above all be yourself. Stay in touch with your emotions while you communicate. If you feel empathetic and warm, allow it to show. Most of the time it will be reciprocated. Showing warmth can be interpreted as having good intentions and being trustworthy.[4] If on the other hand you don't, try and show that you are competent, professional, and objective. Don't try to fake warmth; that will most likely be spotted and mistrusted. Allow a relationship with a champion to grow naturally over time; don't try to push too hard. If you are puzzled by something, ask for clarification. If you feel uncomfortable without being too sure as to why, you may say so and ask how the other is feeling. If you feel fear or apprehension, allow yourself some space to think about what that might be telling you or holding you back from?

4. Communication is not one way

The fourth rule is to remember that **communication is not one way**. Believe us, we do realize that these next few sentences might make you roll your eyes in exasperation at their obviousness. Well, OF COURSE you know all this. But do you always practice it? Especially when you are full of enthusiasm or a new idea, do you really give others the time to digest what you say and do you make sure that they have the space to respond, challenge, and interrogate? Do you jump in and interrupt out of a passionate desire to get your point across? Do you jump ahead because it is your plan and it is fully formed in your head, but don't give your listener the intermediate steps they need to follow? Both Kitty and Shaheena are prone to these communication no-nos. Luckily, we recognize the signs in each other and have such deep trust in our friendship and professional relationship that we can call each other out. Kitty might ask Shaheena to slow down, so she can follow the leaps and bounds of her creativity, whereas Shaheena will ask Kitty to wait until she has explained fully before jumping in with assumptions and questions. We acknowledge this can be frustrating for someone else working with us and trying to communicate with us. We have both had to practice conscious communication and keep refining it – despite being aware and working hard at it, it can be very easy to slip back into bad habits. But one thing we have both become better at doing is calling out this behavior so the other person or people feel empowered to stop us and ask us to slow down or explain the steps.

Your champion is investing in you, so if you ask for a meeting or a call, they will do their best to give you their time. Being respectful of their time and levels of energy, and simple courtesies such as making sure you respect the time allocated, will go a long way. At the beginning of the meeting or call, listening fully to the champion first will help you calibrate what you say. If they are in an expansive, reflective mood and show that they are up for a broad-ranging discussion, then that is great for developing the relationship. In any case, being clear and concise not only makes for a more focused and productive conversation, it makes it easier to be heard and understood.

Remember, human beings communicate with their bodies as well as their words. Pay full attention not just to what is being said, and also not said, but to facial expressions, to movements, and gestures. Respect silences. They give all the participants "time to think,"[5] and they often convey much meaning.

5. Tell good stories

In the introduction we emphasized the importance of leaders being able to **tell good stories**. And we do not mean becoming plausible liars! Storytelling is a key leadership skill and practicing this with your champion is a great way of honing it. Stories follow the pattern used by the brain to lay down episodic memories. Good stories have a timeline (a beginning, middle, and end) with agents (the characters who act in the story) with whom one can identify. Good stories are constructed around a meaning, giving a clear purpose to actions, and a cause for what happens. A good story is also easy to re-tell, giving your champion (and others) an easy way to talk about you and your achievements. Indeed, you may co-create a championship story together, where you both have the material to use in communicating your relationship to others. This can be hugely valuable in certain environments, in order to make championship more acceptable, well-known, or wide-spread.

Negotiation

In order to negotiate effectively you need to understand your own goals and those of the people with whom you are negotiating, an acceptance that in the case of conflict, compromise will be required on all sides, as well as some measure of good intent and clarity of communication.

Communication with a champion is often about negotiating how to achieve a common, relatively high-level goal – your successful career progression. This can be the best basis for negotiation: a championship relationship that achieves its aims is an archetypal win–win. Even if the goal is not your personal career success but, for example, the successful turnaround of a failing division, or the completion to time and budget of a mission-critical project, or entry into a new market, your champion succeeds if you do and vice versa. Although we broadly agree what a championing relationship sets out to achieve, there are numerous opportunities for mismatch. The beginning of a championing relationship will not be formalized with a contract but by communicating: both sides have a chance to express what they expect from the relationship. So you might think that the kind of negotiation skills that are useful in resolving a disagreement or clinching a difficult deal won't be needed, but they are essential. As the relationship and you both develop and change, as your careers progress, your ambitions and goals might also change.

Good negotiation skills can help keep a championing relationship alive and relevant for both of you.

What to do when things go wrong

Championship relationships can go wrong and communications turn sour for a number of reasons. And of course, this is when negotiation skills come into their own. Mismatch of expectations is sometimes the cause of problems in a relationship. Having spotted your potential and helped you achieve the next step, a champion might be keen for you to progress rather more quickly than you are comfortable with. Or indeed you may be very hungry for next opportunities and very excited about the prospect of working with your champion, but in return your champion may see the need for you to pace your progress for your own development and this can cause frustration on your part. Setting out the timescale for your goals early on in the relationship can be very useful for both of you. Making sure you are both clear on what the endgame is and how you each might measure whether you have achieved your aims is also desirable.

Another mismatch can be the expectation of some kind of return on investment for the champion. Most of the champions we spoke to were far from wanting a direct personal gain of any kind, but in some of the stories around championship we did hear of expectations of indirect benefits, even if they were not conscious of them initially. One such expectation could be for gratitude, such that it is not only expressed as thanks, but extended to behaviors that support the champion in a number of ways. Most of these behaviors are likely to arise naturally from pursuing such a win–win relationship, but sometimes the expectations can be excessive.

Loyalty is another way in which a mismatch of expectations can manifest itself. For example, I might think I am loyal if I always speak highly of my champion and seek always to create opportunities to laud their achievements. My champion might feel that it is more about always taking their advice and not having, much less expressing, a contrary opinion. Expressing loyalty can be difficult and may be misinterpreted in different organizations depending on the internal culture. For example, one senior female director in a major multinational, who wanted to remain anonymous, told us that she had been consistently championed by the same person throughout her career in that company, and rose as he did, until he reached the CEO role and she reached the level just below his. With her promotion she was given a company-wide, strategic change management brief. That championship relationship ceased from the moment she told him that she could not agree with one of his policies. The relationship then became progressively more and more difficult until it led to overt blocking of what she was trying to achieve as a change manager.

One of the women we coached had been championed early in her career as a young researcher in a well-known consultancy by her head of division. He had first known her as an intern, and was keen to promote her worth. As her credibility grew, she was sought after for a number of major projects, and her first promotion, supported by her champion, came quickly. Successful now at managing projects, and having considerable in-depth expertise, her work flourished and her own team grew. She developed an external profile, writing well-received reports, being quoted in the newspapers and asked to speak at conferences. Her champion found it difficult to see her as successful and even famous in her own right. To him, she was still the bright youngster he had nurtured and supported through her internship and first career steps. He kept calling on her to work in support roles on projects on which he was the lead, which did not contribute to her learning or continuing growth. Tension arose when she could no longer sustain that workload, along with her own responsibilities. The relationship deteriorated; her champion felt let down. Internal promotion stalled as she was no longer seen as a "team player," so she moved to a more senior position at another company, and her champion felt betrayed. It took years – and retirement – for that relationship to mend.

Out of 60 interviews, only two mentioned a championing relationship that had broken down, so these are exceptions. Being clear about expectations on both sides, maintaining open communications so that expectations can be re-calibrated, being explicit when ambitions change and grow all help. Where relationships are in danger of breaking down, negotiation skills of the highest order MIGHT be useful, if used in a timely manner. We have seen how powerful emotions can be as behavioral drivers, so that feelings of betrayal could effectively close someone's mind. The lack of agreement might be perceived as too big a threat to a position of high status and authority. At the same time, negotiation skills might be effective, especially if the attachment emotions can be evoked. For example, sharing experiences together of joint triumphs in the past where the championship relationship led to the champion's succeeding in their aims can lead to renewed warmth. Repeating and reinforcing the higher order goal of the relationship, the career development, for example, and exploring differences openly can diffuse some emotions. Showing willingness to listen, to find acceptable compromise that will still yield the desired results but perhaps by routes that are not the obvious ones, seeking to understand in depth the other person's perspectives, assuming that both have good intent and there might be right on both sides can all help.

Acknowledging and taking responsibility for one's own emotions and attitudes is a good start to any difficult negotiation. Often our need to be seen to be right can be a powerful driver and one that gets in the way of building a trusting relationship. Remembering the extent to which different people in the same room, in the same meeting at the same time, will see, hear, and remember differently is crucial. What you take away from an interaction will depend on what you are looking for and this may be very different to the next person. For an illustration of this take a look at the Simons and Chabris video.[6]

Exiting the relationship

The championing relationship is not forever. The relationship will change as your roles change. For example, you can remain in touch, but with less time spent on the relationship, as you develop in different directions. You may outgrow your champion and the champion themselves should be first to rejoice in that. If the champion does not share your success and instead starts to perceive your progress as a threat rather than an asset, try to find a way to address that as early as you can. This situation also demonstrates where it can be useful to have more than one champion, especially one outside your own organization.

If the relationship does break down, then at least try to ensure it does so without recrimination and bitterness. Show gratitude, on both sides, for what the relationship has created so far.

Trust and fairness

Trust is a key factor in maintaining good relationships of all kinds, not just between the champion and OTW. Trust is a crucial underpinning of human society. It is the basis of our concept of money, our institutions of government, law, and of the professions. It is trust in our social environment and institutions that permits us to expect to be fairly rewarded for our ideas and labor, to engage in commerce, to leave money in a will, to go to a competent doctor when we are ill.

Developing trust takes time but it can be demolished in seconds. Like belief, trust is a multidimensional concept, hard to define. Most scholars seem to agree that it is a mental action or state, involving relying on another (individual, group or organization, or object) to behave in a way consistent with the "truster's" assumptions and values, in a risky context. Trust is not only restricted to relationships between people, or between people and animals. It can arise between people and objects, such as clocks or tools, or organizations and their brands – I trust my employer to pay me a fair wage for my work, my government to uphold the rule of law, my doctor to have the requisite training to identify a common infection, the bridge over the river not to collapse, my iPad to save my documents to iCloud, Mercedes to provide a car that doesn't fail.

Trust depends on a degree of consistency and integrity between values, words, and actions over time. A champion who opens a career opportunity and says their only concern is your progress but then keeps asking for favors of various kinds might cause you to question their motives. If you accept being championed and being talked about favorably by your champion but don't make significant, consistent effort over time to live up to their words then their faith in you is likely to be eroded. A political leader who builds their brand around upholding "traditional family values" but is outed as having an extramarital affair may have their integrity questioned on other matters. Trust is more easily given to those who seem to have our interests at heart, not just their own. Research has shown that leaders who show self-control are also more likely to be trusted than those who do not. That may be because someone who is more controlled is also less likely to do unintentional harm.

It is said that you do not have to like someone to trust them, or indeed that you do not have to like someone to accept them as your champion. Underlying trust, however, is the chemical neuropeptide oxytocin. Oxytocin underlies a range of human social affiliations and is popularly known as the love hormone, as it floods the brain when people fall in love and when they behave lovingly towards each other, as in bonding between mothers and infants in mammals, or hugging in human adults. It has been shown experimentally that oxytocin can also increase the level of trust in the truster. Administered via a nasal spray, it caused a significant change in behavior during a game played with real money (apparently not linked to lowering risk aversion). Trust, social affiliation, and love are not the same, but an increase in oxytocin levels is implicated in all three. It is possible therefore that an increase in oxytocin in a relationship where trust was developed would also increase affiliation.

A key element in a trusting relationship between people seems to be the concepts of fairness and reciprocity: I expect fairness from someone I trust. I expect our relationship to have a fair balance of benefits for both parties, which may not necessarily mean equal. I expect someone whom I champion to reciprocate my support by delivering on their promises. Trust, then, becomes the basis of a strong emotional relationship, between people, things, and concepts, in which there is a sense of safety and a reduction of fear and risk and perhaps even an increase in liking. This facilitates influence and allows for creativity and innovation.

It seems that fairness, like social contact, is a primary need for humans. The brain responds strongly both to perceived fair and unfair actions and situations. In the first case positively, with the reward centers firing, in the latter case negatively, with those parts of the brain that respond to threats. Humans have such strong aversion to unfair behavior towards them that it overwhelms more rational assessments of the balance between gain and loss. Remember that fairness too needs to come from both sides in a championing relationship. If all the benefits flow one way, then the relationship may not flourish.

Why trust is vital in championship

In order for a leader to inspire and motivate, they need to be trusted and the same goes for a champion. A sponsor might be seen as someone who is more motivated by their career than yours, and that is fine, as far as it goes. But a trusted champion is more likely to elicit true gratitude and a desire to achieve in order to merit their approval and even to delight them by exceeding their expectations. That kind of intrinsic motivation, to be someone of whom another can be proud, rather than to achieve in order to gain a particular status or salary, can extend beyond a single relationship. There is also tremendous reward in being that champion and building a reputation where "I became someone for whom women wanted to work." Being a champion inspires others to perform beyond their own expectations and stretch their potential.

Creating a relationship of trust with someone you champion is an iterative process over a long period of time over which words, actions, and effectiveness are mutually observed and judged. Do words and actions match and is there a coherent set of values evident under them? Are actions fair and effective, if not always, at least mostly? Is there genuine consideration and respect for the other person? A trustworthy champion will be believed when they tell others about what the OTW will achieve in a new role. A trusted champion with a strong emotional commitment to a purpose or overarching goal will be able to engender commitment in those they champion, even when the journey seems dangerous.

An organizational environment of trust is also essential for championship to flourish. If championship is openly accepted and lauded, if women are encouraged to find champions, then individual relationships are more likely to succeed and the company will benefit. Having an overt and clear policy around championship helps develop a trusting environment. The purpose of championship is clearly stated: talent identification and development, improved retention of talented individuals, increasing diversity in leadership, increasing the visibility of talent at the highest levels within an organization, improving succession planning, getting better results in engagement surveys, and improving job satisfaction and career planning – all these can be legitimate reasons for encouraging championship relationships. A few, very few, fundamental rules should be spelled out. For example, senior leaders are encouraged but not required to be champions, and the OTW can initiate a championing relationship, or their line managers suggest one. It is important that championship is seen as a free choice by both champion and championed; it won't work otherwise. Championship is open to all and there are real opportunities for everyone to meet the right level of potential champions for them. By being more transparent and open to all, this type of relationship is far from being like an exclusive "old boys' network," which still exists in some organizations.

Task

For individuals:

This task is about honing your ability to tell a good story about yourself. You know this subject very well but it can be distorted by your perspectives. Find two articles that tell a compelling story about a leader. Do not focus on the leader but look at how the story is built up, what elements are included, how the reader is drawn in, what messages are conveyed? By refining your story, not only are you clearer about what you have to offer, but you will make yourself more compelling for your champion to pitch you to others.

Start mapping out your story:

- What is the message you want to convey about your leadership?
- How do you convey your leadership style? What values do you communicate?

For organizations:

- What would a championing relationship look like in your organization?
- Would you need to create a formal or informal framework for championing? Might you include policy, guidelines, FAQs, case studies?
- If you were to start building a cohort of champions how would you identify potential champions and how would you brief them?

chapter 7

Creating a Brand Worth Championing

Maya has thought carefully about her champion's advice. She recognizes the need to get her priorities sorted and clarify what it is she wants to achieve, and who she really wants to be as a person, at home and at work. Having reconnected with her values, and created a plan of action, Maya is once more able to deliver above expectations at work and focus her time at home on what matters. Her team, peers, and line manager trust her to deliver, but she has been so driven by achieving results that she has not made the time to network and raise her visibility with those above. Some months later, over lunch with an old friend, a successful marketing director for a retail chain, Maya shares her thoughts. Having known her for a long time, her friend offers some wise counsel: "You need to embody your core values, Maya," she says, "and raise the visibility not just of what you do so well, but of who you are as a person and ensure the right people have sight of you. You have the capacity, focus, expertise, and strength to reach the top, but that is not how you are always seen by those who do not know you well – and you need to do something about that."

In this chapter, we are going to discuss the things you need to do that will help you to become part of a successful championing relationship. The right champion will be someone senior who can influence their peers to help promote your career. These are inevitably very busy individuals so your job is to make it easier for a champion to spot you, to know what you are capable of and to understand where you want to go, in other words what your ambitions are. Your leadership brand is the most effective way to demonstrate what Dave Ulrich and Norm Smallwood describe as your "reputation for high quality management."[1] Ulrich and Smallwood described the importance of building a leadership brand for companies in a 2007 *Harvard Business Review* article. They emphasized the need for companies to be able to compete by clearly differentiating themselves from their rival and in doing so move away from what they call "vanilla leadership." The outcome of a clearly defined leadership brand creates a culture of leaders who enhance the values of the company.

Companies seek out individuals whose leadership styles add value to the company brand. But we know in an increasingly busy and overcrowded market, where there is a great deal of talent, individuals with really strong leadership potential can be more difficult to spot. Personal branding is a term that was coined by leadership guru Tom Peters in 1997, when he pushed us to recognize our roles as "CEOs of our own companies: Me Inc."[2] Whilst the brashness of promoting yourself may seem unpalatable, the reality is you are being branded, you have a brand, so the question is, who is in control of your brand? The area of personal branding has become even more important with the meteoric rise of social media impacting how our digital footprint influences how everyone perceives us.

Developing your personal leadership brand needs careful consideration on a regular basis. As you look to develop your brand there are four areas that need attention:

- Your vision and values.
- Your networks.
- How you demonstrate potential or spare capacity.
- Your actions.

Working on these areas is a bit like building a jigsaw – you fit the pieces together and start to build up a picture. This is not a linear process but it is incremental, and you will find you return to each of these areas as they need more refining and as your own leadership journey develops. Before we go on to discuss each of these areas, let's spend a bit of time unpacking what we mean by branding and why it is important to help you develop a championing relationship.

Why do I need to worry about my brand?

You may have identified a senior executive who you would like to champion you, but it's not happening, you are still waiting patiently. Unless you invest serious effort and time into building your brand, you won't be noticed. As customers we have become incredibly sophisticated in our consumption of brands, within a split second we recognize a logo and instantly recall an emotional reaction to it. New brands are thrust upon us on a daily basis and we have the capacity to keep growing our engagement with new and exciting relationships. For any company with a product or service to sell, the only way to create a strong presence and build a customer base in a very crowded market is by creating a strong, distinctive brand. This is where we get the pushback from so many women with, "If my work is good I will get noticed, I don't need the additional layer of branding to get my next promotion." Remember Cinderella and the not-so-meritocratic organization?

Champions are really keen to invest in talent. Remembering how busy they are, it's your responsibility to ensure you are visible to the senior leaders who have the potential to help you move along in your career. Building and developing your leadership brand is so powerful for a number of reasons. It helps you to become absolutely clear about your ambitions and your values. Then as you start communicating to the right people, and we will discuss the importance of networks later in this chapter, you create a path to help you realize those ambitions. For some of you this may sound a bit too uncomfortable, a bit too calculated, maybe? Well, you are all working in organizations, you are all competing for customers to spend money, time, or any of their other resources on your products and services.

No matter how strong your product is, unless you invest time and money in promoting it to the market, how will your customers find out about you? When we talk about branding we are not just talking about self-promotion in a superficial, hyped approach (if you are imagining a bright neon sign with your name emblazoned and flashing lights around the edge). We are talking about you consciously thinking about what your leadership means and how you achieve your end goals. Really effective, sustainable, and compelling branding is about layering, starting from your core, and building the layers. The end product is elegant, well-crafted, and slick, but there is a huge amount of structural work just beneath the surface. We call it creating your Brand DNA.

Your vision and values

Throughout this book we have emphasized the importance of your vision and values and we will spend more time on both of these areas in Chapter 8 on authentic leadership. Building a brand is only meaningful if you have a clear vision, and creating an authentic brand that clearly differentiates you from your competitors will only work if it clearly reflects your sense of purpose. What does leadership mean to you? In other words, what will leadership help you to achieve? This is the big picture we are talking about – what is your imprint on the world? Keep this in mind as you continue to read through this chapter and work on the exercises. When we speak to women who have achieved senior leadership roles they often say, "I didn't have a game plan, I looked for opportunities that were exciting and I took them." Or "I wasn't sure whether I wanted to go for a leadership role but I knew I wanted to do something that made a difference and found ways to challenge myself." The subtext to these comments is mistakenly translated as "I didn't have a plan but hey look where I am as a result of hard work/luck/coincidence/or all three." On the surface, this approach would seem maybe a haphazard or fortuitous approach to the leadership journey of these women. But maybe these women are answering the wrong question, it's not about whether or not they had a plan, the more important question is "what has driven your leadership journey?"

Values underpin the vision you create and we spent time in Chapter 5 discussing how values impact your leadership. We will briefly discuss values within the context of creating your leadership brand. Here we are talking about the most powerful feelings and thoughts you have that intrinsically motivate you. We are not talking about the need to earn an income and support yourself and your loved ones, we are really drilling down to what makes you – well, you. We are commonly presented with values as a way of reinforcing the credibility or authenticity of a brand, often to the point where we become immune to the true meaning of the words and what they really convey. When we run sessions on branding and ask women about their values, their automatic initial response focuses on providing for themselves or their families. On further interrogation we really push the women to question what their values really are, their moral principles or their code of behavior. As the women delve deeper into their values, the themes that emerge are amazingly powerful and inspiring. But, and there is a "but," when we ask the women to align their values to their current role, the connection can break quite dramatically.

Look at the people in your team, you are all working on the same project and operating in the same organization, but do you really have a sense of what differentiates each of you? Could you answer that question about yourself and your colleagues? You hold responsibility for ensuring your colleagues can answer this question about you and not only your colleagues but also senior leaders who may well be interested in becoming your champions.

In the earlier chapters, we spent a lot of time discussing how your vision and values drive you and fuel your ambitions. If you consider your role models or the powerful leaders that influence your thinking, they have the ambition to change things. Ambition is powerful when it is viewed as a force for greater change, bringing benefits to the lives of people. Ambition is driven by values. If you are clear about your values then having the ambition to drive them forward becomes core to your authentic leadership and creates your brand.

For this reason, we place a great deal of importan~~orting~~ with your vision and values when developing your leadership~~nd~~. What is the benefit of a brand? It's a shortcut to convey message~~out~~ a product or service, and really powerful brands elicit emotional ~~r~~ions that either draw us further towards the brand or push us awa~~ys~~ you build the structure around your visions and values, you need to ~~sure~~ they remain clear and form an integral part of your structure.

Through your leadership development you will have a ~~c~~ear idea of your values but when you focus on your personal branding you need to be really clear about how you convey those values. If reliability is one of your core values, how does it manifest itself in your leadership approach? What do you do to ensure you consistently present your values in the way you lead, even when you may be under extreme amounts of pressure or stress? If part of your values set is to empower others to achieve their potential, but you are driven by the need to achieve targets in a very competitive environment, is your leadership style driven by your internal values or by the demands on you as a team leader? In this example, if your team refer to you as someone who gets results at any cost, what does that really mean? If you received that feedback, how would you react to the "brand" being developed around you?

As you develop your brand it becomes easier to make decisions about how you lead, the projects you work on, perhaps even which organizations you will choose to work for. Whatever time you are able to spend on refining your brand brings benefits to your leadership. Why? Because really effective branding is about consistency and alignment between values and delivery. Think about the consumer market, the long-standing brands have survived in an increasingly competitive environment because there is clear alignment between what they say they do and the core values of the company.

Networks

Networks are as diverse as the people within them. We will explore professional networks, the formal structure within organizations, but also consider the impact your personal and online networks. Professional networks that open across organizations and industries can also be enormously powerful. Where these networks operate across different countries the range and scale of contacts for women can be immense. One such example is the experience of Lucy Paine and Vicky Sleight, who met through the GSMA (an association of mobile operators and related companies) Connected Women network. Vicky was responsible for running the network that connected a host of companies from the telecoms sector. Lucy, an apprentice at Telefonica had created an initiative to help younger staff within the company. Vicky was very impressed with Lucy's vision, expression of her values, and clear focus on her goals for this project in Telefonica, despite still being a relatively young and temporary apprentice. Vicky saw an opportunity to give Lucy a really strong platform and championed her into being the keynote speaker at an international Connected Women event. Needless to say, the impact was immense for Lucy, and Vicky still claims that although others saw this as a risky decision, she perceived it as the most inspiring opportunity for others to hear Lucy's vision.

Within organizations, the networks that are really powerful and effective are networks that are multi-layered, providing opportunities for women across the organization to exchange views, learn from each other's experiences, and for the more junior staff to raise their visibility to senior colleagues. Not another call for a women's network we hear you cry, but here's the thing: when set up across the whole organization and managed in an inclusive manner, these networks become a powerful resource to foster relationships, for senior leaders to hear what's really going on and to influence the female talent pool at lower levels and for junior colleagues to learn how the senior women navigated their route to the top. But there are certain behaviors that do need to be challenged; as described by Lesley Stephenson in the UK: "We really need to look at our work ethic. There is an awful lot of networking that still goes on outside of the office, if you are not there. If you are not in the office late at night, it's very difficult for women who are carers to break into that."

Sue Clayton, Executive Director of the worlds leading commercial property and real estate services adviser CBRE UK, described how creating a women's network in a traditionally masculine organization has had a significant impact on changing the internal organizational culture, particularly when attracting female graduates: "You automatically become part of it when you join the company, you don't have to apply. It's mentioned at induction sessions and graduate recruitment centers. It seems to have quite a positive effect for girls at the younger end in what is still seen as a very male-dominated industry." As a result of these networks, senior staff such as Sue are not only more visible but have engaged in supporting and nurturing female talent. The dialogues across the network have resulted in creating a shift not only in the organization but also in their sector for female staff on maternity leave. Previously, when female staff went on maternity leave, their clients would be assigned to a different member of staff and a new relationship would develop. This pattern of behavior made it very difficult for the women to re-establish a relationship with their clients when they returned. With greater openness and a clear expectation female staff will pick up their clients when they return from maternity leave, Sue describes how attitudes in the sector have become more open towards women going on maternity leave and cites examples of much more communication. Networks address a number of issues, providing opportunities for more discussions to share experiences, creating a platform to build relationships across departments and levels and of course raising your visibility.

How do you build your networks?

To build a truly powerful network you need to have a purpose for the relationships you are developing. This will enable you to shape the network and ensure you are targeting people who can help you to achieve your ambitions. None of us lack networks, we all have networks of varying complexity, we are born into networks, and they continue to develop around us as we grow. Family, neighborhood, school, clubs, camps, universities, work, parenting groups, and marriage – each interaction provides a new kaleidoscope of relationships and each network is unique. As these relationships are layered with virtual networks through social to professional sites we have more global reach than ever before. According to the statistics portal, Statista, it is estimated there will be 2.13 billion social network users globally by 2016 – an increase of 1.4 billion since

2012.[3] These figures are astonishing when we consider that many of us think we are too busy to "properly" engage in networks.

Despite the mass of relationships, the missing piece is the quality of networks. Our real challenge is to work out how we can convert the potential in our networks to real opportunities that will help propel our career goals. This is where it starts to get tricky; it means we need to recognize the networks we are involved with have value, but we need to reconfigure how we view these networks and where the sweet spots are, that is, where they add value. When we run sessions on networking in our leadership training programs, we ask participants to map out their networks visually, on paper, or on their tablets or laptops. Without fail in every session, most of the networks will exclude personal contacts, family, close friends, community contacts. Because the context is a work one, our participants are not thinking about their lives as a whole – they are unconsciously limiting their perspectives and yet these are the people who know us really well, trust us, and actually on the whole really want to see us succeed. How many times do we hear the dominance of men on boards and in leadership is inextricably linked to the influence of the "old boys' network" – what is that exactly? The dictionary definition of the old boys' network includes references to relationships generated by virtue of men attending the same school or university who use their positions of influence to help each other.[4] Yet why do women find it so much more difficult to explicitly identify the potential of these relationships for their benefit?

We know that women are, on the whole, more influenced by their social contexts than men. We know again that, on average, women are more motivated by wider social purpose than self-interest. "Women thrive on we," according to Jennifer Crocker of Ohio State University.[5] They feel better about themselves the more they focus on others. Women also tend to be less hierarchical and more participative and democratic in their leadership styles,[6] and also more transformational. Their approach is less transactional than that of men, preferring to provide, upfront, transparent links between rewards and desired behavior at work,[7] rather than giving direct orders. Networks and the kinds of relationships they provide might then seem to be more important for women and yet they appear to be less good than men at creating and maintaining them.

Networks are not static, "once and for all" sets of similar connections. They constantly evolve and will vary according to what we need from them and what we are willing to put into them. We often forget this vital fact and spend very little time really thinking about how we mold our network. Seminal work by Mark Granovetter in 1973 on the strength of ties in networks has shaped every type of analysis since on how we develop and utilize our contacts.[8] Acknowledging that each of our networks will have a combination of deep and weak ties, we also recognize our ability to shift the composition and nature of relationships in our networks. How we use our networks depends on what we need to achieve, and this requires a much more conscious approach to cultivating and nurturing these invaluable relationships as resources. In Chapter 5, we discussed the importance of goals and identifying the resources you need to help you achieve your goals. When considering your network you need to take a really critical approach and work out where these resources sit and what you need to do to shift some of the relationships. You need to evaluate yourself too, properly, as a resource for others in your network. This might take some effort. Once you have located individuals and groups, there are a number of excellent resources to help you identify the support offered and more importantly your next steps to help you build your team. Your actions may well include identifying critical gaps in your network and with this you need the bigger picture mapping to determine who else you could build relationships with.

Championing is a great example of how you can analyze and configure your networks. The right person to become a champion for you needs to have the ability to influence and negotiate on your behalf at senior levels. This means your network needs to be multidimensional with contacts across a wide range of sectors and also across a wide range of levels, including senior and board levels. Some of you may feel this is easier said than done, but the real question is how you leverage yourself as well as your contacts to develop better access to resources of all kinds for yourselves and build a closer relationship with the champion you need.

One of the greatest impacts of social media based networks has been the increased transparency in networking. This helps particularly those who are still building strong networks. It becomes easier to develop and support each other: in the immortal words of Dale Carnegie: "You can make more friends in two months by becoming interested in other people than you can in two years by trying to get other people interested in you."[9] The thrust of this is to enhance your value and ensure you build these relationships from a position of where you add value. If we apply the 80–20 rule to your networks, it is reasonable to assume 20 per cent of your contacts will generate 80 per cent of the value that supports your career aspirations.

What about the infamous six degrees of separation that enable you to have access to anyone you want to connect with? Malcolm Gladwell, who focused on relationships between individuals in *The Tipping Point*, argued that the six degrees of separation is not a literal translation. It doesn't really mean everyone is linked to everyone else in just six steps. But it does mean there is a very small part of the population that is linked to everyone else in fewer, more tangible steps and the rest of us benefit by being linked to these connectors.[10] If you build your capacity and profile to be a connector, and are clearly recognized for the value you add to your network. This in turn enables you to build relations with the higher levels of seniority.

The connector status actually is more suited to women, based on how we build relationships and create networks often motivated by serving others' needs even more than our own. However, we need to ensure we highlight our identity as a connector to reinforce our value and keep growing it in order to become part of that much valued group. As you would expect, there are differences in how men and women use social media. Social media company Brandwatch conducted an analysis on usage of different social media platforms by gender and found men were more likely to use certain platforms to build influence, gather intelligence, and build relevant contacts, all of which increased their professional status. Women by comparison used platforms to reveal more about their personal and social lives. Men are more likely to use professional platforms such as LinkedIn compared to women.[11] For you to use social media effectively you need to decide what it can do for you and how it can enhance your brand and presence. Sharing knowledge on social media is a hugely powerful way of building your presence as a connector and demonstrating your value to part of your network you may want to nurture.

Clearly, social media has considerable benefits compared with physical networking, not least the ability to engage with networks at any time and from any location. However, face-to-face interactions are still crucial in building relationships and this means spending time and effort to be with other people, formally and informally. Attending events can help to build your visibility. To be really effective this means being specific about the type of events; this means asking yourself which internal events will promote you to senior executives in your organization and which external events will build your network for the next step in your career. Remember your peers today have the potential to be advocates for you, even in intensely competitive companies. Peers and managers move and want to demonstrate they have a strong eye for talent spotting.

In an effort to be more resource-effective in handling your networks, a new framework has been developed by Zella King in her publication, *Who's in Your Personal Boardroom*,[12] where she suggests identifying 6–12 key individuals who each take on different roles that will promote and support your career ambitions. There is great merit in adopting a specialization approach for your network and that can be very effective, however we reiterate that the basic premise of your network, maintaining relationships, requires an investment of time and so even with a small, dedicated group a light touch is needed to maintain your network and turn it into a resource.

One of our interviewees described how, when she reached the CEO position, she saw that she would need a group of people to whom she could turn for specific advice, knowledge, or support – not just one mentor or champion. She created such a group and told us she sees them as her own, personal board and an invaluable resource for her leadership.

Implementing your brand

Short of walking around with your values on your t-shirt, your job is to understand how well your colleagues know you and really know what drives you, and more importantly understand what sort of leader you will become. Of course, your actions will always speak louder than words on a t-shirt or anywhere else and if you keep reinforcing them your brand really does start speaking volumes about your leadership potential.

When individuals have a really strong sense of their values and these are challenged early on in their careers, this often creates an indelible mark on their leadership style. Some of the women in this book shared their early experiences, and for some of them this meant taking risks in standing by their values in the face of pressure from others. Naaz Coker reflects on how a conflict of values with a senior manager very early on in her career impacted her leadership: "It taught me you have to take a stand and in leadership positions you cannot forget your ethical principles. You have to make a stand and you don't compromise on your ethics." Catherine Letegele, from Botswana, saw "living up to my values" as one of the greatest contributions she could make as a female leader.

As your brand strengthens, colleagues are more likely to become your brand ambassadors. It becomes effortless to promote you to colleagues who are looking for someone who not only has the skills and experience but also aligned values. As you see this picture building up, you start to understand why a well-defined brand is one of the most crucial stages in building a relationship with your champion. For a senior leader to be your advocate and promote you, they have to believe in you and that means they need to trust you and trust your values and be really comfortable in aligning themselves with you. This is a long-term relationship and their brand will become inextricably linked with yours, so they want to make certain you are credible and a "safe partner."

Developing and refining your brand is an iterative process, in the same way conventional wisdom advises updating your CV at least once a year, your brand needs to be revisited. As you take on new roles, you develop new strengths and skills that can add immense value to your brand. Once you have invested time and resources in developing your brand, the next stage, that is equally important, is to get your brand out there and noticed by the right people. The notion of promoting yourself may send some of you into a cold sweat, but once again we remind you that if you don't draw positive attention to yourself, why should anyone else? Once you are able to clearly articulate your brand and the value you bring to your leadership potential the message is easier to convey.

Raising your visibility

Creating a strong brand is only one side of the coin, you also need to ensure people know about you. We call this raising your visibility. Any well-defined marketing campaign requires a planned approach so you know whose attention you want to attract: in other words who is your "target market?" You need to think about who the key decision-makers are and whose attention you need to attract in order to ensure you build a presence with the right people. You may have colleagues along the way to act as ambassadors for you, but in reality nothing substitutes the impact of having a direct relationship with key decision-makers. For the right champion to find you, your job is to make it easy to spot you. This is not the time for a test of perseverance or playing hard to get. You want to stand out as the person who, in addition to having well-defined core skills and technical knowledge, consistently performs to her values and has the potential to become a great leader. You may not see this in yourself but if your brand, values, and performance are aligned, the impact is powerful.

You as a role model: How is your brand delivering?

Think about a time when you have really fallen for a brand, maybe in your teens or at university or even more recently. You have discovered a brand, whether it's sunglasses, a car, coffee, a mobile device; it could be anything that you see as part of who you are. We are talking about brands that have a strong personal connection and are more likely to be aspirational products that you are happy to be associated with. Once the initial euphoria has worn off, you will keep an eye on the brand, how it is performing – whether it lives up to the hype and also over the longer term how its external image is perceived. The development of the brand's image will influence how you align yourself. If the brand does well you develop a closer affinity with the brand, creating a halo effect. If, however, the brand dips and suffers reputational damage, you distance yourself and may even switch allegiance to another brand. This is no different when we talk about personal leadership branding.

As you take on more senior roles you become more visible. We have spent most of this chapter concentrating on how you achieve this and the benefits it brings to your career. At this point, you need to consider how you maintain and continue to build your leadership brand. Increased visibility increases the chances of you being perceived as a role model. Companies are keen to promote the diversity in their senior leadership team. Graduates making decisions to join companies do their groundwork to identify the presence of women in the company and whether there is a strong route of women being promoted to the top. Men and women in middle management will observe you. Once your brand is "out there" in your organization and your network, you are highly visible. And so by virtue of your effectiveness and promotion to senior roles you will be observed by others, and in particular women, to see how you are doing. This is not about scrutinizing you to see if you are performing, it's about women who want to make that leap and identify others who have done it and learn how they manage. As we said earlier in the book, our research in 2011 showed women actively opting out of their promotion track because they did not like what they saw in their companies – there was no one they could identify with. They did not aspire to that model of leadership.

The media in every country will have a voice that often gives women a hard time if they are working, and will find ways to undermine the value and effort of women leaders. They know the weak spot is to hit at women who are "juggling" too much and inevitably dropping balls at work, at home, in their appearance, or in their personal lives. Women push back to us and say, "I don't want to be a role model, I'm not doing this for the spotlight, I am just good at what I do and I want to enjoy it." None of the women we interviewed for this book had aspirations to be role models when they started their careers, but by virtue of their success they have been propelled into higher levels of visibility and in some cases unusual positions that inspire the next generation of leaders.

Role models are not self-selected; they inspire people for a variety of reasons. The strength of their power lies in their ability to demonstrate a way forward and to help more girls and women aspire to leadership. The diversity of role models creates a broader range of leadership models for younger women. So, as each step of your leadership journey develops, remember your brand, your values and how you want that message to be conveyed to others. Of course, it's more than just about smiling – it's the whole package! When we talk to women on our programs, we often use the example of a swan. On the surface, the swan is one of the most elegant and powerful creatures that glides serenely across the water. From where we stand watching this magnificent bird, its movements are effortless and graceful. However, if we peek just below the surface we see the thrashing and furious paddling of its feet propelling it forward. Consider how this image can be a powerful tool in developing how others view your leadership.

The importance of feedback

Some of the suggestions in this chapter may make some of you feel discomfort, particularly when we apply marketing terminology to you. If this is the case, then try to think about yourself in the third person. We have all had those moments where we provide the most inspirational and constructive advice to a colleague. As you read this chapter and work through the exercises, treat yourself as you would a colleague. Even better, enlist a colleague to help you. Some of the exercises require feedback, so identify individuals who will provide genuine, clear and constructive feedback.

Tasks

For individuals:

Ask three trusted friends or colleagues to align your leadership style to a well-known brand. Each of them should be able to give you a picture of the brand in an advert, to give you a sense of brand impact. Find out why they feel this brand is aligned to your leadership style. Think about the values that these brands represent, for example, Volvo can say "reliable and safe," Rolex "luxury," Harvard "excellence and tradition." The responses will be enlightening and a powerful tool to help you understand how others perceive you. You may not agree with the feedback entirely. This is an opportunity for you to consider your external image and, where you want to, develop yourself to better embody your brand.

Keep these images and add your own, create a mood board to keep track of how you want to develop your brand. Visual stimulus is powerful, so keep the mood board picture somewhere accessible near your desk or on your phone or laptop. Identify opportunities to refine your brand and build your profile for greater visibility, for a champion to recognize you and identify a fit.

For organizations:

- What does your brand say about diversity in your organization?
- Can you enhance your brand values and messages to signal that you welcome and support women in leadership?
- How else can you convey messages of inclusivity to potential recruits and your own staff?

chapter 8

The Power of Championing: Unleashing the Power of Female Leaders

Fast forward five years. Dara has retired and is now Chair of an International Development charity, and Maya is at the helm of the company as CEO. She has gained an enviable reputation within the industry for her strong individuality and tenacity, attracting the best people to work for her. She is adept at encouraging her people to develop their own unique leadership style. She has made significant waves in the company and is largely responsible for the surge in retention of women. Maya has reached the pinnacle of success. Things couldn't be better for her. She takes a moment to reflect on the last decade or so and recalls the great angst and confusion she had once experienced and how one relationship had set her life on track for the success she now enjoys. She looks up and offers silent thanks for that moment her champion walked into her life. Her thoughts are interrupted by the telephone ringing and Maya smiles as she receives yet another call from her champion …

To some degree or other, women everywhere face barriers to flourishing and achieving their potential … Globally, women also tend to be locked out of leadership positions, where gender seems to matter more than ability. The benefits of greater inclusion are clear – not just for women, but for all of us. For a start, women are the ultimate agents of aggregate demand, accounting for 70 percent of global consumer spending. So if we want growth, let us put women in the driver's seat … We also know from the business side that prejudice does not pay. Companies that are open to women do better than companies that are closed. For example, the Fortune 500 companies with the best records of promoting women have been shown to be 18 to 69 percent more profitable than the median firm in their area.

Christine Lagarde[1]

We began the discussion in this book with Christine Lagarde's keynote speech delivered in Japan in 2014. She argued that one of the most important levers for improving the global economy and accelerating its growth is to "unleash the economic power and potential of women." We urge you to read it if you haven't already done so. Like Lagarde, we believe that including women around the world equally in the labor markets would be a powerful engine for growth. Also like Lagarde, we believe that it is not just equal numbers of women at lower levels of the economy that matter, but equal numbers of women in the most important decision-making positions in international institutions, governments, the public sector, and all kinds of businesses. Commentator Moises Naim observes: "For Lagarde, appointing women to positions of authority is not just a matter of fairness. She genuinely believes that women tend to manage power better than men. And she hasn't been afraid to say so publicly. I read her some of what she has said on the record about this issue: women are more inclusive managers and are more inclined to create consensus; they are better leaders in times of crisis; they are better at managing risks and juggling tasks; they pay more attention to detail and at the same time have a more holistic view of life."[2]

That is why we believe championing women is critically important: because it is such a powerful lever for accelerating women's progress into leadership positions. Championing is a powerful force for good, not just because of fairness or inclusivity, but because enabling more women to take leadership positions can make beneficial changes at global, national, organizational, and family levels – both economically and socially.

It used to be said that in order for a merger to succeed, the DNA of both organizations needed to change. Well, for championship to succeed, the relationship needs to change both champion and championed, and also change their environment in some way. Successful championship relationships need to be given the time, space, and right environment to grow organically. If the right level of trust doesn't develop, the relationship will not generate the energy and power it takes to make profound changes in the individuals, their organizations, and their wider environments.

We are not saying that all women make better leaders than all men, or that all leaders should be women, but we are saying that a diverse mix of people at leadership levels is better for all kinds of organizations and institutions.

It is not only the championship relationship itself that is powerful, but its side effects, the way it is seen and felt by others outside it. For example, championship by the most senior directors in an organization can act as an influencer or attractor in the hugely complex combinations of systems that make up a human organization. That is to say, the behavior becomes noticed and copied by others, because it looks like an integral part of the values and processes of the organization, an unspoken "this is our way of making sure our best people have a chance at the best jobs," "this is just the way things are done around here to develop and retain the most talented people," and so gets embedded in the culture over time.

What does female leadership look like?

> Always remember that leadership is nothing unless those who are led give the best of themselves. Like love, leadership is, at its best, about giving not taking.

These words, written by Dame Stephanie Shirley towards the end of her autobiography, were inspirational for us.[3] They come from the heart and reflect the unique combination of character, mind, and experiences of one of the most creative and authentic women we have ever met and learned from. They reflect perhaps a vital source of power in female leaders and champions alike, their ability to get the best from others.

Stephanie (Steve) Shirley is an entrepreneur and philanthropist whose work is recognized as pioneering in both fields. This is a woman who made it in that most masculine of worlds – IT; who changed her name from Stephanie to Steve so potential clients would agree to see her; who made millions from her enterprise … and yet who is flamboyantly, triumphantly, herself – female.

Be your authentic self

As we said in the introduction, there is no single model for success as a female leader. But one thing we learned from all the successful women we interviewed was that, in order to succeed, they had to be themselves … to find their own way or ways of leading, to create their own leadership style and brand. In order to have power as leaders, they had to have authority and to have authority they needed to be authentic.

They did not use that language; in many cases this finding of their authentic style of leadership was not a consciously-planned search, it was a natural heuristic development of themselves as people as much as leaders. For others, it was a deliberate iterative process of developing their skills and capacities. As Catherine Letegele, CEO of Botswana Life, told us: "The greatest contribution I can make to the next generation, is to teach them the value of being your authentic self, the best person you can be is yourself, so be self-forgiving, be open to new ideas, network with likeminded individuals, most of all accept your imperfections and leverage your strengths."

Authentic is perhaps an overused word these days, but we are using it to mean original, genuine, authoritative. In terms of authentic leadership, we mean a way of leading which belongs to you, as an integral part of who you are as a person, which you have developed and in which you are the authority.

And in saying "a way of leading" or "a leadership style," we are using these terms as shorthand, condensing all the behaviors, attitudes, capabilities, knowledge, and personality traits that make up your array of leadership behaviors. We do not believe that people have or should have only one way of doing anything. As Daniel Goleman said in his famous article, "Leadership That Gets Results,"[4] leaders need to be able to deploy a variety of styles depending on circumstances. A sinking ship, literally or metaphorically, requires directive, coercive leadership: "Do what I tell you and don't stop to question my orders." Building a knowledge-based business most often needs a combination of authority, inspiration, and a democratic approach.

Creating your own form of leadership

So what does it mean to create your own form of leadership? For us it starts with **knowing and understanding your values**. Your values are the drivers of your behavior, for good or ill, so being clear about what they are helps you understand why you do what you do in response to various internal and external stimuli.

Secondly, it is about **knowing what you want to achieve**, for yourself and for others, your goals and the purpose and meaning you want your life to have. Knowing your values and aligning your goals consciously with them gives you purpose and meaning with a cohesion and integrity that other people can sense. Being able to express that purpose and meaning powerfully, in the form of a personal vision and mission or a story, can help motivate yourself and others towards achieving your goals.

Thirdly, it is about **developing self-awareness** and self-reflection, understanding your strengths and weaknesses, recognizing your defaults, your attitudes and biases, and being motivated to change and develop: to increase your strengths and address those weaknesses that get in your way. We agree that it is beneficial to focus more on your areas of strength, to develop these into practices and traits that demonstrate your value, and to spend most of your time in areas in which you can apply them. But we also believe that addressing those weaknesses which prevent you from being the best you can be, can be a strength in itself.

You cannot be perfect at everything – no human can be – but you can change, develop, and improve your attitudes and behaviors. So it is also about creating and re-creating yourself.

A NOTE ON SELF-REFLECTION

We know that women do tend to focus more on their weaknesses and less on their strengths than men, so we recommend self-reflection to aspiring female leaders with caution. Self-reflection is not self-flagellation; not dwelling on mistakes, not ruminating on what went wrong. Self-reflection is as much about taking some time at the end of the day or the week to acknowledge what you did well, to make a list of what you are good at, as it is about recognizing you need to boost your confidence and stop publicly attributing your achievements to luck. Of course, it is also about learning from your mistakes and others' mistakes and taking that knowledge forward. We think about self-reflection as a way of getting to know yourself better, as a way of gradually growing your capacity to see yourself with some measure of distance, of giving yourself feedforward as well as feedback. Having a champion, someone who is "on your side" and to whom you can turn for objective, positive reflections is a great way of calibrating your own self-knowledge.

For many women, owning their strengths and achievements is hard. They seem to need more external affirmation to break the habit of modesty that has been inculcated in them since nursery school. That is where championship can help enormously in resetting that internal dial from pointing to "don't boast" to "it's ok to be happy and proud about what you've achieved."

Fourthly, it is about **understanding and tuning the impact you have on others**. Being sensitive to the feedback you get from the people around you, as much from their physical behaviour as their words – but not so sensitive that it can completely derail you from your own values and purpose. This is about understanding your personality and how you react to others as well as how they react to you. Are you powerful because people willingly follow your lead or because you can give them orders? Do they understand and embrace your vision? Are you perceived as authoritative? Competent? Do people pay attention when you speak? Is your stance confident and authoritative or hesitant and apologetic? Do you come across as driven and stressed or in control of yourself and your time? In our work, training women for leadership, we help them understand that sub-conscious biases play a big role in how they are perceived by others – and in how they perceive themselves – and that how they present themselves and communicate – ALL THE TIME – can be adjusted to help overcome bias.

What does authenticity mean for me?

In our coaching and training work, we often found ourselves responding to the question, "Do I have to dress/behave/think like a man in order to get taken seriously as a leader?" Or even, "Do I have to become like a man in order to gain a senior management or leadership position around here?" And when we say, no, of course not, unless that is part of who you are, naturally we are challenged to explain how women can escape from the double bind of bias, without compromising their authenticity.

Sabrina had a champion who showed her, by example, that you could be a feminine woman and a leader: "BW really allowed me to be me. The relationship I had with BW enabled a sense of self – authentic self – you did not feel the need to be so guarded. I learned it was OK to be a woman. What I wore, how I looked wearing color and being able to stand out – that was the transformation. When I reflect, the foundation is an unconscious bias – in both men and women. I have just watched a couple of women present and one was nervous; women don't think about talking too quickly or that their voice might be too high, therefore people dismiss women easily and that creates a vicious cycle. I don't think women make enough effort to talk in a way that men can relate to; well thought out, slow, logical, not high pitched. I managed to fit in my thinking on communication, what I needed to impact that particular audience.

It was coming together, I had the knowledge, learned about people, how to inspire and motivate those who don't have to do what you say."

We have seen many women leaders who exemplify Sabrina's message: you can retain your individuality and femininity and be convincing and powerfully authoritative, if you plan and tailor your communication to your audience. They recognize that communication is hard and that the better you understand your audience, their assumptions, and needs, the better you will be heard. This is as valid for men as for women, and effective communicators and leaders know that and spend time practicing. Your core message, your leadership story, may be the same but it will be delivered differently to different audiences.

Crafting your image in a way that not only expresses who you are as a person but reinforces your unique brand is also part of how you communicate – and that can be a constant. Look at Camila Batmanghelidjh, founder of the Kids Company in the UK, which supports over 36,000 children, or Chanda Kochar, Managing Director and CEO of ICICI Bank, who constantly wears a sari whether working in India or addressing delegates at Davos. These women present themselves in a way that does not compromise their individuality, femininity, or their purpose.

Amanda Nelson, CEO, said, "We genuinely value diversity here. Women want to be authentic. And be themselves. I know I want to be collaborative, intuitive, and that you will get the best of me like that. Not allowing women to be themselves puts them off, they see it as a lack of integrity. Some women don't like the tough stuff … The integrity piece is crucial. I am not going to lead in a masculine way. All humans have strengths and weaknesses. It's up to us to set the bar."

Your version of authenticity will be your own, and different to mine or Sabrina's or anyone else's. It may take some time for you to find your own way of being, to find your own sources of energy and power, to determine your own vision and the stories you want to tell around it; how you present yourself, how you brand yourself, and how you train yourself to be effective with different audiences, especially in the early stages of your career, when you have not yet perhaps had time to have a full range of relevant experiences. Remember to practice, to try out different approaches, gauge their effects, and listen to feedback.

This is where a champion, with their wider experiences, can be helpful, both as a role model, but especially if they offer a safe place and audience of one for you to practice with.

A new model of leadership allows for diversity

Our model of leadership is relatively straightforward but profound: it is a unique combination of the following:

- Who you are (your personality, values, beliefs, and experiences – and how you use these).
- How you think (the quality, effectiveness, and efficiency of your mental processes, combined with your level of expertise).
- What you do (your mental and physical behaviors and your self-management capacity).
- How you relate to other people (your levels of empathy, trustworthiness, and openness).

This model is based on the neurobiological model of leadership first put forward by Kitty Chisholm in 2015 (see Figure 8.1).[5]

In our modern, knowledge-based society, leadership power is not just about giving orders that are obeyed just because you are stronger or have the right title. One of the key features of our model is that it is one according to which there is no single kind of leader. Another key feature is that this kind of leadership can be developed throughout life; it is not an innate characteristic of certain kinds of people. People of whatever combination of color, ethnicity, gender, physical capability, and faith can fit this model comfortably.

It is based on the thesis that, unlike in dominant higher primates, leadership in human beings is not simply correlated with high levels of testosterone, but also with the ability to manage stress in particular, and to

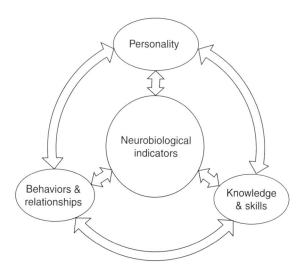

FIGURE 8.1 / A neurobiological model of leadership

manage yourself more generally. The key to leadership where you are leading brains is being trusted, and trust is strongly correlated with self-control, not high levels of testosterone-fuelled aggression, competition, and risk taking. We have also found that leaders share certain characteristics with experts: they are better able to see patterns and meaning, they see them faster, they can chunk information, and assign probabilities more accurately.

Leaders develop the ability to focus their attention on what matters and to change that focus very rapidly when they need to. They use intuition and rationality appropriately in taking decisions and are open to new ideas and inclusive of new people with new ideas. They put effort into their relationships with others and seek to understand their perspectives.

We know that you can change yourself by changing your brain, by developing new connections and pathways, and practicing the behaviors that embed them. In order to better manage stress and hence reduce cortisol levels, you can develop a number of strategies that increase your resilience. For example, sudden unexpected exposure to extreme risk – such as on a battlefield or, in peacetime, a threatening, aggressive bully – can be very stressful, but if you lead up to it by exposure to situations which gradually increase in risk or danger as you become trained and able to handle them, your resilience can increase. Just like confidence then, early exposure to stressful situations and challenges at work, to managing people (during which you have the right training and support, from a champion and your organization), can prepare you for leadership. And that means, given the right opportunities, women and men of all kinds can become better able to manage their stress.

The same holds with self-management more generally: the wider the range of testing experiences you have, with the right level of learning opportunities and support around you, the better able you will be to practice self-management in ever more testing situations.

Entrepreneurial leadership

We believe that leaders, like entrepreneurs, are better than managers at managing their responses to risk. We noticed a number of women within our sample who recognized risks, but saw the opportunities in them more clearly; who did not hold back but consistently said yes to opportunities, trying out new things and pushing the boundaries of the possible. These women did not always have an idea of the outcome of their efforts or ventures, and they did not always know how they would do it, but they knew something needed to be done and they would do it regardless of both risk and uncertainty. Some of these women were entrepreneurs, crea-tors of businesses, others saw themselves as social entrepreneurs, creating non-profit ventures to benefit their community or a particular part of soci-ety. Others were creative or disruptive forces in conventional businesses. What we saw clearly demonstrated by these women were behaviors strongly aligned to entrepreneurial activity. These include: high internal locus of control, a high need for achievement, and the ability to manage risk, albeit calculated risk. These characteristics seem to be independent of culture; seen even in strong religious or collectivist cultures.

We have noticed a growing number of female entrepreneurs, many of whom, like Steve Shirley, are turning away from a safe salary in a large organization to create structures that better suit their own lives. We also noticed these entrepreneurial behaviors in women for whom conventional routes to senior positions seemed blocked, who wanted to be the boss, so they either set up their own company, or headed up an independent unit, working below the radar to run their own operation within a larger organization.

Individuals who demonstrate a high need for achievement are also individuals who keep pushing the boundaries of what they want and what they expect for themselves and from others around them. Entrepreneurs, both women and men, are often described as people who are unreasonable in what they expect, and although this can seem like a criticism it is also a characteristic of visionary, inspirational leaders. They may seem unreasonable as they drive others to fulfill a vision that only they can fully understand. These are individuals who not only can see the bigger picture others cannot yet grasp, but who will challenge the status quo, disrupt markets by creating new products and services; who seem to know what consumers and clients will want before they know it themselves. These are the people who continuously drive innovation throughout their organizations. It is often argued that entrepreneurs do not make good managers, and we have worked with enough entrepreneurs to broadly agree with this statement, although we've met some extraordinary exceptions too.

Risk tolerance

Being a leader who innovates and challenges boundaries requires an appetite for risk, a tolerance of failure, and the ability to bounce back from it. It requires confidence to change the norm and move into the unknown. Increased risk tolerance is correlated with raised testosterone levels. Indeed, it is often said that women are more risk averse than men and that their neurochemistry could be an underlying reason for this. This relative aversion to risk is one of the characteristics that is meant to make women worse leaders than men. For example, you may hear that women hesitate too much as leaders when times demand quick and decisive action in high-risk situations, and some commentators attribute board reluctance to appoint women to the very top jobs to their perceived inability to handle risk. On the other hand, since the global economic crisis, there have been a number of calls for more women at the top of financial institutions for the very same reason, their risk aversion, on the grounds that their lower tolerance of risk would enable them to achieve better results in times of turbulence.

Although a number of studies have indeed found that women are more risk averse than men, the evidence is not clear cut. Women seem to be more influenced by context when assessing risk. There also appear to be some differences in how men and women react to ambiguity in decision-making, which might also affect how risk is assessed.[6]

Susan Fisk, of Stanford University, in her paper, "Risky Spaces, Gendered Places," put forward an interesting thesis: that women's attitude to risk is in part shaped by how women's performance is perceived by others and in part by a tendency to be more anxious about risky situations. The tendency to judge women more harshly she found to be a factor in *perceiving* women's performance in risky situations, defined as those with uncertain outcomes, which have the possibility of resulting in either significant gains or losses, as worse than men's. This might then play a part, over time and with repetition, in women choosing to avoid risk, by perhaps increasing their anxiety around it,[7] thus fulfilling stereotypical expectations.

If men and women assess risk and ambiguity differently, this difference could be of value in itself as part of the process of decision-making, enabling different perspectives to be evaluated. This difference could thus be one of the reasons why a gender-balanced board and senior management team is correlated with improved organizational performance.

It may indeed be that women are more risk and ambiguity averse before they have had time to build up their personal experience of success. Again, this is perhaps another reason why championing women early in their careers is so effective. It enables a perspective based on the champion's track record of success to be applied to career decisions. A number of our interviewees spoke of having taken personal risks throughout their careers, and how they were often encouraged and persuaded to take them by a champion. We also heard a few stories of champions selecting women to promote because they would be innovative, creative, entrepreneurial, and disruptive. Annie Mary Ruth, New Zealand, says, "I consulted my business manager, and decided to make the Head of Directing an Associate Director – he was a Māori, but then some members of staff complained to the Board behind my back and I had a huge ruckus with the Board. My job was on the line, but the Chair supported me. There had also been an increasing use of Tikanga Māori (doing things right the Māori way) in the curriculum and some people thought that had gone too far."

Jan Owen, Australia, states: "Risks? Everything was a risk. I made it up as I went along. I went to the top people in Australia to get them on the board and camped out in their office until they saw me and agreed. I always backed myself and the work."

Time and time again, we hear companies demanding we include innovation and creativity as part of their leadership programs. They want to encourage "intrapreneurial" behavior in their organizations, but in reality they do not want to pay the price. Their processes are geared to minimizing risk and reducing the chance of failure. They fail to recruit, nurture, or retain the people who will make change happen. Risk and failure are part and parcel of the innovation process and the organizations that provide resources and "space" for experimentation, exploration, and failure are those that can really truly achieve creative and innovative solutions that will create new markets or dramatically increase results. Yasmin Jetha describes her approach to encouraging her team to take risks in deeply conservative organizations and Jane Cummings describes being supported to deliver great change in the public sector: "I had some very good peers and colleagues and some good bosses. They gave me the OK to try out different things and develop ideas and new ways of thinking. When I went to the NHS Modernisation Agency, I was a member of a team looking to make changes and I knew a lot about this and I had ideas about how to do things differently and enable them to become policy and I got promoted above my boss's boss. I ran the programme and we delivered massively, we were supported by people who recognised I had value."

The creativity and innovation allied with the nurturing qualities and inclusive tendencies of female leaders may be a more acceptable way of introducing valuable, sustainable innovations.

Championing female leaders across all levels in large organizations and bureaucracies may prove to be the most powerful force of all. This may indeed be the key to unleashing the true value of women's leadership – enabling them to release their own *and others'* creativity and innovation.

The power of female leadership

Crucial to the success of championing is its output: a powerful female leader, capable of improving the performance of her team, her division, her company, or country. Such a leader is capable of managing risk, of inspiring trust in others, of a strategic perspective that enables her to see beyond most people's boundaries, creative and entrepreneurial, and above all able to influence and motivate others to achieve an innovative common goal.

The most obvious benefit of including female as well as male leaders at governance and senior executive levels is simply that they will see things differently. Being an equally good leader does not mean leading in the same way. Women use their brains in different ways, their bodies and life experiences are different. Diversity, as we keep reminding you, is good for business and good for innovation. Diversity of perspectives and experiences help to combat bias and thus leads to better decisions. New and challenging ideas that cross disciplines and jump over silos cause discomfort and provoke more probing thinking. They can present new problems or old problems in new ways that demand creative rather than familiar solutions. We have in this book argued primarily for gender diversity because we see this as "low hanging fruit"; one of the quickest and easiest ways for organizations and states to improve their economic and cultural well-being, but we believe in championing diversity of all kinds.

Having said that on average men and women are more alike than they are different, what specific benefits do women bring to leadership? A number of articles published over the last few years argue that a more feminine style of leadership is more suited to the kind of organizations that flourish in a modern, super-competitive global economy, where the key resource is the power of brains, not bodies. An article authored by Jack Zenger and Joseph Folkman in 2012,[8] debating the merits of female versus male leaders, had some interesting numbers. Using data from 360° evaluations,[9] they surveyed 7280 leaders on 16 competencies. Interestingly, although the study confirmed, as expected, that women were perceived as better than men in those competencies which are traditionally seen as more feminine and nurturing: relationships, developing others, self-development, and showing integrity, it also showed that women were perceived as better leaders overall. Surprisingly, women were perceived to be even better leaders than men the higher up the organization they were. Even more surprising, they scored higher in two competencies that have long been seen as stereotypically male: taking initiative and driving for results! In view of what we know about unconscious bias we wondered whether, when judging a particular woman or a particular man whom you have known well over a period of time, your judgments are less colored by gender bias and more by how you perceive their actions and how you relate to them as people.

Our own research showed that women, on average, do bring some specific benefits to leadership. They are more likely to **consult widely and seek consensus**, which is especially useful in flat organizational structures such as partnerships, and in organizations where the power is not held by management but by expertise, such as academic and scientific research bodies. Women are also more **motivated by a "bigger purpose"** and by delivering wider social benefits, which can mean that their drive is more for the organization to succeed than for their own promotion or glory. We also found that they are **motivated by helping others to succeed** and that trait means they are more likely to build strong teams and develop people capable of being leaders across the organization, creating a dispersed leadership structure, which helps build resilience in times of uncertainty and turbulence. That is perhaps why women also make good champions.

Women leaders are **more empathetic** and, as aggression is inversely correlated to empathy, they are indeed, confirming the stereotype, **less aggressive** than men. Finally, they are **more focused on people** and tend to have a **more inclusive approach**, which leads to more diverse teams.

This is far from saying that women can now coast, their case is proven, they don't have to work so hard, and they do not fall into the traps of hubris and overconfidence, like any leader. What we are saying, however, is that it is worth investing in championing women, because female leadership has the power to benefit your organization, however large or small, and whatever its purpose. There is a way to go to achieve a critical mass of female leaders but with the right inspiration it can be done, as a female board member from Canada states: "Female leaders of today – if you can see it maybe you can do it. The 4-minute mile – for thousands of years no one could do it, when the record was achieved, many people reached it within months. Before Roger Bannister achieved this no one thought it was possible."

The power of championing is not just in increasing the number of female leaders, and accelerating their career progress, but in the wider advocacy for diverse leadership, for promoting talented people even if they don't fit the current leadership stereotype of male, tall, deep-voiced, white, and fit. Championship is a powerful lever because it addresses issues that are deeply personal and individual, such as confidence and bias, as well as organizational culture, issues that have been traditionally impervious to change through more conventional methods and processes. It is in essence a natural relationship based on values of equality, belief in human potential, and trust; a powerful relationship capable of accelerating the growth and development of human beings.

Tasks

For individuals:

The "As If" speech – this chapter started with a powerful quotation from Christine Lagarde's keynote speech. Every leader is marked by their ability to convince others to join them in creating their big picture. Your champion needs to hear your big picture and your job is to convince them to support you on this journey.

So take some time to imagine your pitch – whether a full keynote speech or a shorter sound bite. If you love the opportunity to act out and remember role playing as a child, this a wonderful chance to really step into your emerging leadership style and practice your speech out loud in private, to your partner, your children, or close friends. If this makes you feel uncomfortable, play it in your head a few times – what would you look like, where are you standing, how are you standing, what are you saying? When you have finished – stop, breathe, and remember how it feels to be speaking and sharing your vision with those who want you to succeed.

For organizations:

- Develop and write down a vision of what increasing the number of female leaders might deliver to your performance?
- Who would you need to involve to do this?
- How can you best share that vision with your key stakeholders?

9

Case Studies

Anne Abraham, CEO, LeadWomen, Malaysia

For Anne Abraham, the timing was right. It was 2011 and the Malaysian government had just announced a goal to have 30 per cent of all board positions filled by women. She had been CEO of Cisco Malaysia for three years and was asking herself what she really wanted to do in the next phase of her life. Having moved up from a technical position to become CEO of two businesses – she previously had the role at SAP Malaysia – she "thought it was good for me to reflect and capture some of the things that had helped me to get there and help women realize their own capabilities to get them there."

And so Anne established LeadWomen, a company with a mission to help coach and prepare women to take senior leadership roles in the corporate world. The key was getting businesses to collaborate and change their mindsets on the value of gender diversity on their boards: "The government set an aspirational goal and not a 30 per cent quota, to give this matter focus, which I believe, is the way forward. After all, this is a business issue and not a women's issue ... The first challenge was to build the supply," she says, "to train the women, and the next step was to create the demand: to make sure the companies that are looking for board directors look at this ready pool of supply." There is enough supply for the first few years and now "it's looking at how we grow that demand."

So far, around 800 women have participated in the Women Directors' Program, in which LeadWomen was instrumental in designing the framework and delivering on 80 per cent of the courses. The network they are creating will create a momentum that will naturally bring more women on. It is, she says, about "women helping women; I think this program has created that mindset amongst women. We say openly, women are their own worst enemies at times. We talk about sharing an opportunity. Once you have one or two board positions, share the third one around and give other women the opportunity who are ready to go. Change should start with us, this is the way we will see the numbers get higher and share the mind shift. We need strong women networks that can really share and help women to get to the next level."

LeadWomen was really a turbo-charged version of what Abraham had been doing anyway, as a keen mentor of young women. "While I was in these [senior] roles a lot of young women would come and ask me about my career, how I navigated it, whether there were glass ceilings," says Abraham. "I had a lot of these kinds of questions from women in mid and senior management. So that motivated me to get involved with women in leadership forums, and sit on panels representing the views of women in leadership."

Her own success, she acknowledges, came out of being championed. "In the early part of my career I never really identified them as champions, but in hindsight I can see even from my very early days they believed in me and gave me the opportunity. They didn't know if it was going to work or not," she says. She was brought into strategic roles that were about business growth. "Those were the opportunities that really gave me some amount of visibility in the market," she says. "As you get visibility because of that, and when the market gets to know you, that's when recruiters start to look for you for strategic organizations."

So what does she look for when picking someone to champion? "Usually it was the right attitude, someone willing to try something different, to step out of their comfort zone, and that x-factor that you just cannot describe! A lot of women were dedicated but you had to convince them to step out. Men are more open to risk and are willing to take on roles that they have to work to fit into, unlike women. With women you had to work hard to build them and nurture and help them to get ready to step up and take it." Championing can't be too structured or there is no space to grow, she says.

"Some people feel you are being biased. I reply – no, you are seeing some unique potential in this person and create opportunities for this person to grow but it goes both ways. You do need to step back and say: 'I am giving everyone equal opportunities, but in this individual I see that special talent and I want to grow and prepare that individual.' These are the very individuals that can build resilient transformative organizations and we need them." She continues, "I am an ambitious person. I never ran up and said I want to be a CEO, but you look for strategic opportunities to prove yourself, and when you do that and you are successful you raise your visibility at the levels that matter for your next move. So it is about: delivery and performance and merit, take the visibility when you have the opportunity and clearly understand where you want your dots connected going forward."

And her advice to those who want to champion? "They also have to reach out a little harder to women," says Abraham. "Let them know I think you have the capability, make it easier and reach out to these individuals. People should come forward a lot more."

Franceska Banga, CEO New Zealand Venture Investment Fund, New Zealand

When Franceska Banga was advised to train as an occupational therapist on the grounds that it was a "good career for a woman," it was the start of quite a journey. She became head of department in a teaching hospital, aged 23, but after a few years decided that her career prospects were limited and returned to university. An economics and finance degree led to a postgraduate scholarship from New Zealand's Reserve Bank and an economist job at the Bank.

There, the "progressive" departmental head recognized that too few women were in senior positions and sent several on a course. "Women had to learn strategies to break through the glass ceiling. It sounds so easy!" But it wasn't, of course. "Many of us concluded that at that time the ceiling was reinforced concrete." She learned an important lesson: "That was a good insight because then you can make the choice to work in organizations that are more supportive."

Time at a private sector economics consultancy led to a senior role in the Ministry of Health, with responsibility for health service delivery. This led to a job as director of the health sector budget at the Treasury, "a male-dominated environment," where she led a major project on organizational culture and change that resulted in the Treasury developing strategies to retain and support capable women to progress. Since 2002, she has been CEO of the New Zealand Venture Investment Fund, overseeing $300 million of investment capital for the country's technology companies.

One valuable lesson she learned in government was to speak her mind. At one critical point, she remembers, "I didn't think it was right to take a 'Yes Minister' approach, given the stakes," and told the Minister of Finance her views, which were counter to those of her colleagues and to what the Minister wanted to hear. "It was a big risk. Well, he didn't take my advice, but I didn't lose my job. I like to think he respected my boldness and integrity!"

This was an important insight, she says, and was influenced by her husband, a colleague at the time. "In those days, I didn't always have the confidence to express my views, in case I was wrong," she says. "His approach was, 'Where there is insight there is responsibility to speak out.' That really changed my approach – I understood that if I wanted to have influence, I needed to be comfortable expressing my perspective and sharing insights."

"I had a fear of looking stupid or being rejected, but the more I have practiced stepping out of my comfort zone, speaking out, sharing my insights, the easier it has become. I've built up a track record – I've taken this risk before and it's been well received." This is especially important in governance roles. "I have a responsibility not just in a fiduciary sense, but also to proactively add value through the insights I bring to the table," she says. "I'm not a passenger."

"There are still quite a lot of invisible barriers for women to take on leadership roles," she thinks. "Especially when it comes to women being appointed as directors of public companies." Barriers are real and varied, but "I also think a lot of women hold themselves back: I think that for women one of the most important things is to believe in themselves, back themselves, get the support they need to get ahead, build their own confidence and strategies for success. A lot of the barriers I have faced are internal," she says.

What helped her overcome these? "The mentoring I received (including from my very supportive husband) and the specific leadership courses I have attended." She also benefited from reading about personal growth and the power of attitude and mindset. "I reflect on my own attitudes and actions that hold me back," she says. She recently took courses on public speaking, an area she perceived as holding her back. "I fronted my fear and found the tools I needed to overcome it. My attitude to public speaking has completely changed, I really enjoy it now!"

Does she champion other women? "I always say yes if a young woman entrepreneur seeks my guidance or advice," she says, and she works with Global Women, giving workshops tailored for women. She also "encourages and advocates for the women within NZVIF who are interested in building their own leadership capability. I am very comfortable to advocate on behalf of other women, seeking board or other leadership roles."

One area women should improve is using networks. "Women are great networkers and we support each other in many spheres of life – but we can learn a lot about how men build their business networks and affiliations," she says. "Successful leaders build strong networks of influence and support. I think many women are so busy forging their own career path and balancing that with family life that they haven't had the time or seen the value in supporting each other on the way through, and developing their business networks. That's an area where we can do a lot more to support each other."

Anne Bouverot, Director General GSMA, UK

After completing an engineering degree in telecommunications and a PhD in computer science, Anne Bouverot started working in Mexico as an intern at Telmex, the country's fixed phone provider. At the time, it was being privatized and the winning bid was an international consortium that included Grupo Carso, Carlos Slim's company, which was taking its first step into telecoms. Bouverot was in charge of looking at the IT processes and systems.

Over the next decade she worked in the enterprise sector of telecoms on many projects, including submarine cables laid under the ocean by ships. Another job took her to the US, near Washington DC. She managed teams across the globe – in the US, Europe, and Asia. "Then I moved to mobile," Bouverot says. She became Chief of Staff for Sanjiv Ahuja, the global CEO of Orange in London. When France Telecom acquired Orange, she became head of the mobile service business unit for France Telecom Orange, which included managing the mobile business across about 30 countries in Europe and in Africa. Moving to Orange was a pivotal moment in her career. "It was a big change for me, as I went from being responsible for a P&L, with hundreds of people reporting to me, to a role where I was on my own, with a very open-ended scope," she says. "It was a very different role from running a business unit because you are not officially in charge of anything, yet you have huge influence on many things. It was a good learning experience, and also gave me the opportunity to see how a CEO operates and works on a daily basis."

Bouverot says that France Telecom's Barbara Dalibard, who was in charge of Orange's business division, "always was a strong role model for women." But she was a rarity. "When I started out, women in technology fields were definitely not the norm and there was probably not the focus on creating gender parity that there is now," she says. "I wish that there had been. I certainly make sure I spend some of my time now to help other women in this field."

In 2011, she became Director General of GSMA, a body that represents the interests of mobile operators worldwide. "This is a very exciting time in the industry, as already half the world's population is using mobile services, and this will only accelerate in the future," she says. Throughout her career, Bouverot has been involved in several networks designed to increase gender parity in telecoms and ICT. The GSMA has a Connected Women program, which aims to close the ICT skills gender gap, to attract and retain female talent and encourage female leadership in technology globally; and to "increase women's access to and use of mobile phones and life-enhancing mobile services in developing markets."

She adds: "Women may pause their career paths for a variety of reasons, whether it's to start a family or care for a parent, and in some cases it's hard to get back on. It's not impossible to do both, but I think for women, there's an added pressure from society and also from ourselves to be perfect – and that's an important thing to realize, that you don't have to be perfect. It's enough to just be good."

Jayne Bryant, Head of Engineering and Technology, Defence Information, BAe Systems, UK

Jayne Bryant says she fell into engineering. Her story is deeply embedded in that of the company she works for, BAe Systems, itself a product of a major merger with Marconi and parts of GEC, and later a JV with Finmeccanica, a company whose products and services cover air, land, and naval forces, as well as advanced electronics, security, information technology, and support services. An archetypically macho world, you might think.

As a young woman, Jayne chose a software engineering role at Marconi, combined with studying for an HNC. Aged 21, she had 15 mainly graduate engineers working for her and a job where she felt valued. Very soon she was being given problem projects and was "getting stuff out of the door" on time and to budget. She moved more into systems engineering and even more challenging frontline roles.

In 1993, she had triplets – a challenge of a different sort altogether – and when she went back to work, still recovering, the company supported her by offering her a different role, working three days a week for the technical director on large complex projects. Jayne feels that perhaps the rigorous organization and tough mental and emotional discipline you need to cope with looking after three babies at once meant that juggling that with part-time work made it seem easier.

Five years on, she went to work in the corporate headquarters, working in a quasi-consultancy role. It was another interesting challenge: from working supported by teams, she had to learn to do everything herself, from gathering facts together to writing reports and presenting business cases. However, she soon felt stuck in a career rut, seen as a "working mum"; she was so keen to get back to the frontline as an engineer. Her next role saw her returning to her old division, which had changed considerably due to various mergers and takeovers. She realized then how much she cared for the company and loved that kind of work. So much so, that she had to fight to remain objective when she first moved back. She moved around the business taking on different roles and now in her role as Engineering Director, Jayne is the most senior female engineer.

The business has changed its culture enormously since Jayne started in 1976. "You had to be tough to survive and sometimes had to be aggressive to be listened to. Wolf whistles, Playboy calendars on the walls, behaviors that would be subject to lawsuits now, no one would get away now with what I went through." Now there is flexibility, D&I policies and a whole support network for minorities, from minority networking groups to an ethic hotline.

Priming the female pipeline is still hard, though. Jayne mentors a lot of women, having herself had the experience of being mentored, informally, by someone who was a great sounding board for her. She persuaded the company to allow one of the women who worked for her to come back part-time after maternity leave, something which is far more common now.

Jayne feels that the biggest barrier to her own career progress was "being seen as a working mum." On the whole, being a woman was not a disadvantage: as there were so few, if you were good you stood out. She was entered for an award and interviewed by Valerie Singleton early on, which gave her a high profile. She has continued to build her profile and is a role model for many younger women, not only in her own company but also, through her membership of her professional body, in other companies too.

Her advice to women coming into the profession now is that what they need most is the confidence to believe in themselves, in how good they are, and to trust their instincts. Her own career was built on taking opportunities, so for her, mapping out your career from the start feels a bit strange – her recommendation is "take opportunities as you go and jump into them!"

Tracy Clarke, Director, Compliance, People and Communication, Standard Chartered Bank, UK

The power of a champion is nowhere more evident than in Tracy Clarke's story. Tracy began her career at Standard Chartered 30 years ago in 1985, as a gap year choice before heading on to university. "I had no aspirations to be a banker. I didn't know what I wanted to do. I wanted a year out before going to uni. I answered an ad in a local newspaper for a bank I had never heard of. I got the job and never looked back." As she built up experience in Nottingham, Tracy decided not to start her university degree program but continued at the Bank.

Further career opportunities led Tracy to Birmingham and on to London. Her career progressed as a result of different opportunities and the growing recognition of her potential: "It wasn't an intentional start – it was by accident: the variety and diversity of the job, having some good managers and mentors who had invested in me, and I furthered my academic qualifications part-time." In London, Tracy recognized she needed to work internationally in order to progress her career: "My husband is a big traveler and entrepreneur. He saw an opportunity for me to stay with Standard Chartered and a chance to travel to Asia."

Tracy and her husband spent a couple of years in Hong Kong and this enabled her to develop a good understanding of what Standard Chartered was all about. She started studying for a distance-learning MBA sponsored by the Bank. During this time, she developed a critical relationship that shaped the rest of her career. Her mentor during her MBA was Mervyn Davies.[1] "He was amazing for my career, he encouraged me it was possible to be a good mother, a good wife, daughter, to handle family commitments but at the same time have an enjoyable and successful career. He saw talent in me and gave me confidence that perhaps I didn't have." When the couple returned to the UK, they decided to start a family.

When Mervyn Davies became the Group CEO he approached Tracy Clarke for help. He needed someone to run the CEO office. Tracy gave him a list of talented names but, "he asked why my name wasn't on the list. I said I had a three-month-old baby and a two-and-a-half-year-old: I said it wasn't great timing, but he said don't be ridiculous you'll make it work." Tracy took on the role and in her words, "it was the best thing I ever did. It was very exciting."

Tracy did the role for a few years, then Mervyn Davies approached her again and told her she needed to do a bigger job. Once again, Tracy pushed back and said, "I can't, I have never run a function before, he said don't be ridiculous of course you can." After that, Tracy made a concerted effort to focus on herself; "I started telling myself – look, focus on your strengths, you are where you are because of your strengths. So I started to take a different approach to my career, this became my underlying philosophy." This approach paid off and Tracy was then asked to lead the Human Resource function for the group, and she took on this role along with her existing Corporate Affairs role. In 2005, Tracy was holding a role on the board of a subsidiary company that Standard Chartered bought in North East Asia. Once again, Mervyn Davies saw the potential for Tracy to step up into a board role in a FTSE 250 company in the UK and he championed her for a board role with Eaga plc, which she held between 2007 and 2011, then moving to the BSkyB board.

Tracy's willingness to take on new roles is now far more evident. She was offered the chance to run compliance at Standard Chartered and, recognizing this was a big risk, she embraced it: "I'm not a lawyer but have loads of general business experience. There's experience and skills that I don't have, but I aligned myself with good people; so I was happy to give it a go." Tracy is clear about her work ethic and the values that have shaped her leadership approach and career success: "Half finishing something is never good enough for me, what I did I was going to do well and finish it. I'm incredibly focused and achievement oriented – that's made a big difference throughout my career."

Sue Clayton, Executive Director, Capital Markets, CBRE, UK

"Real estate is very male-dominated ... about 30 per cent of graduates entering the industry are female so numbers are improving, but it's still one of the last bastions of old boys' networks. Gradually that's breaking down, but there is still bias in some pockets, or maybe unconscious bias." Despite her candid admission and having been at CBRE for over 30 years in several challenging roles, each having contributed to her knowledge, growth, and expertise, Sue notes that without making swift decisions she would not be where she is today. Fifteen years after joining the company as a fresh-faced graduate, Sue earned a partnership position in the company.

"I have changed my role a few times, that has kept me interested. Because I have been on our boards I have been able to contribute to the growth of the business over all of those years." For Sue, the biggest stretch came at the time when she was promoted to equity partner, which required a unanimous vote, so she relied heavily on endorsement and advocacy of her peers. It was no small feat in a male-dominated arena and Sue clearly acknowledges the role her backers played in her success: "It was a combination of me planning and them supporting me. With a partnership, if they bring in a new partner, everyone dilutes their share so everyone needs to be convinced the new partner is going to contribute new business and therefore it is worth them diluting their stake."

Sue's success and inclusion at the highest levels of the organization was consolidated when she was invited to sit on the CBRE Group Inc Board. This was yet another stretch scenario as it was her first experience of an American board, and Sue demonstrates beautifully how a great attitude and belief in her ability held her in good stead: "Being a publicly quoted US Board, there was a lot of regulatory and governance stuff that I wasn't familiar with." Sue prepared and anticipated for the position, all of which put her in a strong position. "I had two or three very good induction sessions with our American chief counsel on the legal side and our European chairman was very helpful ... I had also spoken to Americans who had held the position before I accepted the position, to understand what was expected."

It is clear that Sue has real tenacity and is unafraid of taking risks: "I also decided rather than carry on doing investment deals I would step back and focus on our strategic client relationships ... That was a big step change away from doing deals and billing big fees towards growing our key client relationships, which are not as visible to the firm. But I wanted a change." This begs the question, who was the biggest influence and how did she manage to become so successful in such a male-dominated environment with a notable absence of female leaders? Sue describes it as being a natural process of championing rather than a formal sponsorship: "If a leader has two or three good people in their team they will encourage them, even if it's not formally stated as sponsorship. They will nurture them. I've done it in my teams, if people are good and you want to fast track them through."

Having reached the very top of the organization, Sue is proactive in championing both junior and senior staff and she does a lot of this for women. There are more women coming through but not nearly enough: female role models in leadership positions are especially in short supply. This makes it all the more important that leaders like Sue make a real impact and devote time and energy to advancing women through the ranks.

Speaking about barriers for women in leadership roles, Sue maintains that she has not experienced that glass ceiling at CBRE, but accepts that organizational issues can count against women in certain circumstances: "The lack of senior female role models is quite a challenge, if younger women can't see role models they find it worrying and think 'well is this the place where I want to be in five years if I want to start a family?'" Recognizing the importance of her position as a role model, Sue is very active in the gender diversity arena. As one of the founders and Chair of the CBRE UK Women's Network, Sue speaks compellingly: "I think female role models are a big thing, but also demonstrating an absolute belief that their careers can flourish. I want lots of people to have the opportunities that I had."

Naaz Coker, Trustee, Royal College of Obstetricians and Gynaecologists, and NED, National Audit Office, UK

"You have to take a stand and in leadership positions you cannot forget your ethical principles. You have to make a stand and you don't compromise on your ethics." For Naaz Coker, her early experiences in the NHS as Director of Pharmacy shaped her determination to do the right thing, whatever the consequences. Despite being raised in colonial Tanzania, with a culture of injustice prevalent in its society, Naaz would not be swayed in her resolve to do the right thing.

Naaz has taken a stand on injustice throughout her career and notably when witnessing prejudices in public service she was conscious of not allowing it to permeate her mindset. "I would be rubbished and people would say you're OK, you're one of us." At the Kings Fund, Naaz went on to undertake a big piece of research on racism in medicine, which was turned into a book. This has remained a constant feature in a career in which she has worked hard to include variety, depth, and subject knowledge.

As Naaz thoughtfully puts it, "You need to get the support system in place, get your facts right, don't stay shallow around issues, you have to go in-depth around issues." With her obvious tenacity and will to succeed at full throttle, Naaz firmly puts herself at the center of her belief not to wing it but to demonstrate that you "convey knowledge and you have weighed things up."

Naaz is clear that you need a strong support system in place when tackling prejudices in the public sector and that staying within ethical boundaries takes real courage. She recounts how she relied on her husband, friends, and colleagues, particularly women, to get her through the difficult times: "In all my difficult situations it was the women who have helped me to get through these issues, taking risks, making a stand." One of the strong support systems she had in place emerged in the form of Baroness Elaine Murphy, who she says had a huge impact, especially at the time she was facing ethical challenges, despite facing leadership challenges of her own! Among her team of supporters, including her mother and friends, she has relied considerably on the support of champions throughout her career of 40 years, of which she spent 39 in leadership positions. Indeed, it was a consultant at The Marsden who said in support of her application, "we are going to back her for the pharmacy promotion." Champions have played a significant role in progressing Naaz's career and she remarks poignantly, "It is hard to get around. People are not all bad, not all men are against women, and not all women are against women. You need to have the right network to get a different perspective."

With her friendly, extrovert personality, Naaz insists that maintaining visibility is a key ingredient to being successful, as she has clearly demonstrated. As Chief Pharmacist, she found herself at the management table, which gave her some great exposure, and not being satisfied in that role she explored other things. "I volunteered to do different things to maintain visibility and build capabilities beyond my profession. You need to make yourself visible, take risks, and step out of your comfort zone. It doesn't happen easily but it happens."

Leadership and self-awareness have played an important role in all of Naaz's career choices, and as a leadership and executive coach she has developed her own style, perfecting it to a fine art that she employs in steering others. She highlights the importance of knowing yourself and your weaknesses. "If you don't know yourself, what are your strengths, your problem areas, it will trip you up all the time."

Sabrina Dar, General Manager, Cisco, East Africa

"By chance I saw a lady I had worked with before … I just happened to see her and talk to her over a coffee – completely by chance – and she said 'Don't leave! I can give you a job involving travel.'" Sabrina was about to make the worst move of her career when she happened to have a conversation that would significantly change the trajectory of her professional life. Sabrina admits that conversation and ensuing opportunities enabled her to learn a great deal, leading to the GM position that she currently holds. Of her decision to stay, she exclaims, "I loved, loved, LOVED it! I sat next to her and learned. I had no job description and I built that job from scratch. It was she who put me onto an accelerated leadership program – which was a transformative experience."

Her natural curiosity and appetite for learning has served Sabrina well. From her first role at Cisco as a finance graduate to the present, Sabrina has acquired an astute sense of defining what she needs to do in order to succeed: "I realized I had to do things quickly to make an impact. I continued that learning for five years, became the most junior analyst reporting to the most senior. I didn't always 'sit at the table', but I didn't mind that as I was learning about seniors and developing teams." Working at an EMEA level gave her a different learning experience, being exposed to senior decision-makers and their thinking. Absorbing everything around her as she went along, building on each experience, Sabrina went from strength to strength. "It was almost as though I was gaining confidence in getting knowledge. I wanted to apply it – writing skills, facilitation, all the skills of business leaders."

Sabrina identifies the impact even the most difficult relationships had on her learning and her overall experience, showing great resilience and objectivity in her approach. Of her time at EMEA working in the strategy team, she recalls almost fondly, "My boss there was the first woman I worked for but I found it the most difficult and the most rewarding relationship. I still use the learning today. I truly believe that 'you can learn as much from a working relationship that you feel easy and natural, as well as one that you don't (perhaps even more)'."

The striking thing about Sabrina is her absolute determination for authenticity and it ultimately took female role models to give her the confidence to demonstrate this in her day-to-day working life. From being comfortable talking about shoes, as well as being open to understanding how men think, and adapting her style to relate and so have a discourse that is a meeting of minds rather than a stilted exchange. "I don't think women make enough effort to talk in a way that men can relate to – well thought out, slow, logical, not high pitched. I managed to fit in my thinking on communication, what I needed to impact that particular audience." Interestingly, it was one of her champions and role models, Bernadette Wightman, who gave her the most insight into how she could develop her authenticity and be comfortable with projecting her true self without compromise: "Bernadette Wightman really allowed me to be me. The relationship I had with her enabled a sense of self – authentic self – you did not feel the need to be so guarded. I always thought and planned before meetings, how to keep a poker face. I have relaxed a lot and trust myself to reach out based on good feelings, and while I still need to prepare, I can now carry things without." Sabrina now assumes a natural stance and experiences little intimidation to conform in any way: "I learned it was OK to be a woman. What I wore, how I looked wearing color and being able to stand out – that was the transformation."

Equally, Sabrina acknowledges a number of men in her environment who shaped, sponsored, and encouraged her in her career. From being given opportunities and praise to "tough love" and great feedback, which fed her awareness, emotional intelligence, and vision. "What these men did was allowed me to sit in their meetings – mind, I was earning my seat at their table – and I could listen to them and learn from them." Her advice to future generations of women leaders is one she's learnt through her own experience of working with her role models: "Show that you can be a lady, a woman and do this job. You don't have to stop wearing colors, building relationships the way you do, to do this job, you can be you, you can wear high heels if you truly deliver and you have to be confident about yourself in order to deliver."

John Donovan: The Champion's Perspective, Cisco, UK

John's name came up on a number of occasions as someone we needed to speak to. He was described as a proactive and successful champion for women. John has successfully championed seven women who have gone on to become directors, and amongst this cohort two became VPs and two became senior directors. That was enough of an endorsement for us and we tracked him down for an interview. For John, championing is clearly about talent: "For me the acid test for whether I sponsor anyone – man or woman – is whether I am willing to stake my reputation on someone else's, whether I would advocate them at the risk of my reputation."

All of his championing relationships evolved informally. Building a relationship is critical for him and he knows the value of investing in the individual will generate far more awareness about their potential and is then more likely to invest himself by "putting myself out there."

When spotting talent he is very clear it comes down to one thing, self-belief in their own abilities and potential. In his experience, men and women at junior levels are likely to have the same levels of competence and experience but there will be significant differences between the genders in their self-belief. John is clear about his intervention: "I think my role is that I've got them to believe in themselves – and I think that is what they would say too. They (OTWs) have to change and build their confidence and that takes time. I do it by pushing them to do uncomfortable things. I needed to push them – with a safety net but without mollycoddling them."

John has worked out the approach he needs to take, telling someone they need to be more confident will not usually yield behavioral change. In his experience, encouraging them to be more courageous and giving them practical examples is far more effective. Getting them to do it for themselves is a sure-fire way to success. He is a strong advocate of promoting peer-based feedback. He uses this approach as a powerful way of acknowledging leadership development and in doing so is also building these essential skills. He approaches this with the same degree of tact and firmness and pushes back when the OTW dismisses any praise, with negative comments such as "they are only saying it to be nice."

The basis to his championing relationships is to break it down; the first step is to instil and reinforce the baseline of confidence. Having achieved this, he then works on raising expectations. He finds by constantly challenging the mindsets of the OTW in terms of their self-belief and conviction in their ability, he notices a tangible change in their confidence. As their confidence grows, they take greater ownership over their career development and are more likely to push themselves for more demanding opportunities. He sees the turning point when the OTW not only starts to push themselves but also starts demanding more challenging opportunities.

He acknowledges this process takes time and patience, and the amount of resource required in this relationship means he has to be sure about the risk of investment. In supporting and promoting women into leadership positions, John is very clear about their model of leadership: "you have to be yourself, regardless of style or gender. For example, there are some feminine men and some masculine women, and whether feminine or masculine you have to be yourself, not gender bound. The more you act a part, the less authentic you are and you need to be authentic to be a leader."

John is also very clear about what he gets out of the championing relationship: "I find it personally fulfilling at a spiritual, emotional level. Helping people and seeing them thrive is its own reward. It helps me broaden my network inside the company. For example, A is now a VP in the US and she often calls to say that she has been talking about me and what I do – that can't be doing me any harm. It is more that I enjoy the challenge of seeing someone see themselves as someone bigger. I know what kind of player I want to be, so I invest time in coaching both men and women. Every amount of time I put in I get back, because I have raised the competence of my team."

Carmen Rosa Graham, Management Consultant and Board Member, Peru

Carmen is part of a large Peruvian family. The very basics of her character – her love of hard work, her values, the things you "can't study" – came from her upbringing and her genes. Her parents were very supportive, preparing her for the top university in the country. After an initial stint as a researcher she moved into business and "was lucky" to be hired by IBM in 1981, as there were very few professional opportunities at that time in her country. She was hired to be trained as a systems engineer; which required continuing her professional studies at IBM and holding a job. Carmen made good progress and, having graduated as a systems engineer, spent the next 23 years at IBM.

Carmen's responsibilities grew constantly, as well as her career promotions, and she became a manager at IBM after five years of experience. In 1995, she was given HR regional responsibilities across Spanish-speaking America. She needed to be convinced to take the role as she was not in agreement of HR practices in the region at that time. This turned into a transformational change management role for the next two years. Her roles at IBM created a number of new opportunities. She was always being offered new experiences: the first woman in sales, the first woman country general manager. The President of IBM became her champion and offered her important opportunities at the beginning of her career; he was so clear about her career trajectory and advising her on how to manage various corporate protocols.

When she had finished her stint as GM in Peru, she was asked to move to Florida, but her family resisted. Instead, she was given the role of Director of Strategy for the region, but after a while, she was asked to move to Brazil and she decided to leave IBM in order to stay in Peru with her family. She developed her interests further into the realm of governance, to be ready for the next phase of her career, in various board roles. In 2006, she was elected President of Universidad del Pacifico, her alma mater, and she also serves on the boards of a number of high-ranking companies, advisory committees, and not-for-profit organizations focused on education. Carmen believes that rotation is a healthy practice in boards and personal development, and has been true to her belief.

Carmen recalls that life as a businesswoman in Latin America could be challenging, although things have changed in a positive trend. A lot of business was discussed after hours or in social events which were mainly attended by men; sometimes it is difficult for a woman or mother to participate. Work and family dues were very demanding so there was not a lot of time for socializing. "There were no nurseries, no places for the under-fours; childcare was either families or hiring staff, which at times could be dangerous – and we had to live with that."

When she was appointed GM at IBM it was seen as a breakthrough, and Carmen herself became a role model. She is modest about her own efforts to promote women; in governance she has put effort into securing equality in senior management and building pipelines, as well as her work as part of Pro Mujer and founding professional women organizations in her country (Women Corporate Directors – WCD, and Organization of Women in International Trade – OWIT). Carmen's advice to young women working their way up now is to "go for where you can find flexibility and have NO FEAR of new experiences. Know what you like and want to do, exceed expectations and say no when something doesn't work for you. In the old days, some entrepreneurs might say, 'Who needs women? We are doing so well as we are.'" She feels the younger generation of men and women recognize the value of diversity more, and are making small changes in board behaviors.

Carmen recognizes there are still barriers that need to be addressed; women step back from making a commitment to a top job that means sacrificing too much family and personal time, not only during longer working hours but in the after-work networking. She also recognizes that many larger organizations are much more political, and that women don't always like to play politics: "we like to talk things through, but once we have decided, we just want to get on and do it."

Leigh Gunkel-Keuler, employed by a leading pharmaceutical company operating in South Africa

As Public Affairs, Policy and Communications Director for one of the world's leading pharmaceutical companies operating in South Africa, Leigh Gunkel-Keuler has more than earned her enviable position at the helm of one the world's largest brands in corporate South Africa. Her career started in the performing arts as an intern projects coordinator before she moved through many different promotions. It was in the early 2000s that her career trajectory would take a dramatic turn. With a post-apartheid democratic regime taking shape, funding for the arts was withdrawn and Leigh had to make a huge decision and moved into commerce. It was a decision she would be forever grateful for. She secured a position with one of the leading Chambers of Commerce & Industry (CCI) in South Africa. She was employed as a Senior Manager for Marketing and Communications where she learnt a great deal about the local economy and the macroeconomics that underpin it. Retrenchment forced a huge leap of faith that completely changed the course of her career.

Having spent almost five years at the CCI, Leigh became extremely knowledgeable about the provincial landscape, provincial government and how that translates into the building of a vision. Then came the international exposure which strengthened Leigh's next role, as CCI was such a flat structure there was little hope of vertical progression. Leigh moved and secured a position at one of the largest private hospital groups in the country as Regional Marketing and Communications Manager for up to 16 hospitals along the coast. "It was a wonderful opportunity for me to get what goes on in the private healthcare environment, and to apply what I'd learned in the CCI to the benefit of the industry, in terms of the rotation management, stakeholder engagement."

As one of the youngest candidates for such a senior role at that time, Leigh's regional director expressed concerns that she would be poached in no time at all. True to form, just two years later, Leigh was snapped up by head office to work at a national level and found herself moving to Johannesburg to take up the role of General Manager of Marketing and Communications for the group. It was around this time that her career effectively wavered somewhat: "I was ready for a directorship but it wasn't forthcoming. The company recognized I was ready for promotion and a directorship but they wanted to pace me. You know sometimes you have to believe in yourself." Although Leigh was unhappy with the state of play she decided she would use the GM role as a stepping-stone and worked wholeheartedly to do the very best she could while she was there. "I had concerns you bring a black person into a senior management role and then you don't fully empower them. Being a black individual and a woman, I felt I was being blocked on so many levels and my potential was being stymied. So I took the position and I did some great stuff for as long as I was in the role."

By this time, Leigh had been working for some 13 years and was feeling unclear about her future goals and career planning. She knew what was needed and took a year out to really connect with herself and establish her goals. It was a full nine months before she returned to the workplace in her next role, "it was as though I had given birth to a new life, it was my maternity period." Just four months into her role at this leading pharmaceutical company, at senior management level reporting to the Public Affairs, Policy and Communications Director, she was asked to take up the position of acting Public Affairs Director when the Director resigned. She was eventually appointed into the Director's role and became part of the leadership team. Leigh is very clear about the strengths that are critical at this stage of her career and articulates what is necessary for anyone in a leadership position: "If I go to an organization, I immediately think about what I can bring to that organization as a value proposition based on what/who I am: that needs to be evident very quickly. I have to react very quickly with a clear focus on the short term and what I can bring to the problem. It is so important to have the leverage and credibility outside of your business, seen as thought leaders outside of your sector."

Yasmin Jetha, Board Member, Nation Media, UK and East Africa

"Diversity is an incredible strength when you get capable people with different backgrounds working together. But diversity, like any resource, needs to be harnessed and cultivated carefully." For Yasmin Jetha, diversity has been a central theme throughout her career and board appointments. She has worked in IT across different sectors. Her career in banking took off with Abbey National (now Santander), where she stayed for 18 years, holding 11 different roles. She then moved to the *Financial Times* as CIO and later COO (and member of the Executive Management Board), followed by five years as CIO and member of BUPA's executive team. This diversity is mirrored in her previous roles, including higher education with the University of Bedfordshire, and in her current role as board member for the Nation Media group across East Africa.

Working across a range of sectors helped Yasmin build a strong base for her career and enabled her to create a strong leadership presence, adapting to different environments. Whichever sector you are working with, Yasmin stresses the importance of having a clear strategic vision for the organization and aligning goals: "Once the vision is developed, it is important that everyone can see how their goals are aligned with the vision. And these goals need to be audacious as this stretches you and your team, and enables the company to be competitive."

Yasmin is clear about how her teams needed to work in order to achieve success: "What you need to succeed is not just self-belief but belief in the power of the team." She recognized her role as a leader in setting the environment for her team; "I've always liked to work in dynamic environments but I have learnt to deliberately go slowly initially in order to go fast overall. This means thinking and planning in a greater detail upfront. My experience is that you end up delivering your goals faster and so it's not about 'pace' at the very beginning but 'thoughtful pace' which is sustainable."

Yasmin's appetite for "risk" developed early on; six years into her role at Abbey National she was offered her first executive position beyond the IT function, with responsibility for 1500 staff in over 20 mortgage service center locations. The role entailed travel, which was a challenge for Yasmin who had two young children: "I hesitated, of course. This was a much bigger role in an area where I had no previous experience. But I was also excited about the new role, and after considering the advantages and disadvantages, got used to the idea of a steep learning curve. This was a turning point in my thinking on what I was capable of achieving."

After a run of successful roles, Yasmin became an executive director on the main PLC board within Abbey National – the first female in its history. She then moved to a different sector with the *Financial Times*. "The media sector is a dynamic and fast moving environment where the product has to be totally refreshed every day and there can be many editions a day. Whenever there was a systems problem, whether at midnight or a weekend, there was no time to be lost. It had to be resolved and almost instantly."

Her track record of achieving goals provided the momentum for Yasmin to push even further. She encouraged her team to aim for bigger and more challenging goals, even when she acknowledged the risks were high if they failed. "By setting stretching goals you may miss them (and risk being blamed by your seniors) but you achieve a lot more than if you set goals which are easy. Going for Big Hairy Audacious Goals – beyond stretch – unleashes immense creativity and potential within yourself and also others."

Yasmin is methodical about how she approaches a new situation; "The first thing I do in any new role is assess the current state, without being judgmental about the past. I am not interested in finding scapegoats or cover-ups, just dealing with the situation as it is. Then focusing on the outcomes by setting stretching goals, getting alignment of all stakeholders, board members, staff, other departments on the goals and the plans. And then unrelenting focus on execution." She is clear about the importance of self-belief and stamina, that build the resilience to handle the inevitable setbacks, and she is consistent in this approach: "It's a formula I've used again and again, and it has worked for me."

Yasmin benefited from developing a close working relationship with champions and when the opportunities emerged she didn't need to be asked twice: "I grabbed them with both hands." She in turn now is committed to providing support to the new wave of talent coming through the workplace and recognizes the value she has to offer: "It is heartening to hear from my ex-colleagues, sometimes decades later, how much they learnt working with me. I feel the opposite – I feel I have learnt and benefited from the experience of working with every single colleague over the years. We are all unique and have our own special perspective of life."

Candace Johnson, Entrepreneur, founding President, Europe Online Investments, Founder Global Board Ready Women, Founder/Co-Founder, SES, Europe Online, Loral-Teleport Europe GTWN, Succès Europe, France

At the age of five, Candace Johnson was given a model of the Russian satellite, Sputnik, as a Christmas decoration. At the age of six she had her own transistor radio, at eight she was talking to the world with an 80-year old ham radio operator. At ten, her father – General Johnny Johnson, the first Director of Telecoms and Communications Policy in the US government – spoke to her class about the moon mission and how space would enable us to communicate and educate. Communication made possible by satellites would bring peace in the world, he said.

Peace may not yet have come, but Johnson has spent her life educating and communicating using satellites. Having studied music (she has five degrees, no less), her first venture was to use satellites to beam classical music programs across the US. She was 23.

Aged 28, she married Luxembourg's ambassador to the US and moved to his native country where she set up the satellite company that would become Astra, the world's biggest. In 1991, she started Teleport Europe, Europe's first independent private transborder satellite communications network, and three years later

Europe Online, which enabled Europeans to receive Internet-based interactive entertainment via PCs and television.

The businesses she has set up have been estimated to have a total value of $15 billion. Now she is using satellites with a mission. The Oceania Women's Network uses satellites to connect a number of remote island nations and groups, including the Cook and Solomon Islands and New Guinea. Another project, Laser Light, combines optical lasers with satellites to deliver broadband access without needing radio frequencies. "This could be the largest internet backbone for the world, including remote areas which currently have poor access," says Johnson.

Who inspired her to embark on this amazing career? "My father was a huge influence," she says. "When you are an entrepreneur, doing something no one else has done before, it is very important you have someone to talk to who has no hidden agenda and who can be there for you. That was the case with my dad. I could speak to him and ask questions and know he had only my interests at heart." Her mother's support mattered, too. "We don't talk about our mothers enough," Johnson says. "She was love personified. No matter what I did she always thought it was wonderful and she always believed in me."

Has she faced hurdles in her career? "I don't see barriers," she says. "I realize that a lot of women had not been as fortunate in having the doors open, the opportunities to learn and experience that I had," she says. "I was born into a family where doors were open. It never occurred to me that I was a woman or that something wasn't possible. I do not accept no, even in little things. I never noticed that I was the only woman even when I was – and was often, too. But I never thought about it. The fact that I didn't think about it helped me. Sometimes I became 'the woman in the window', the quota woman. Then I thought, I have a tremendous responsibility to do the best I can so that the doors are open for other women."

To that end, Johnson co-founded Global Board Ready Women, a database of 8000 women who are ready to take board positions. She thinks that "the current criteria for boards are not conducive to including women from non-conventional backgrounds, including entrepreneurs. They too need both quantitative and qualitative criteria. You can learn how to read a P&L, you can't learn not to give up."

Johnson chose not to have children, but her message for those who do is "please come back to the workforce, we need you," although she acknowledges that "society needs to make that easier for you." She highlights the story of Sandra Day O'Connor, who graduated at the top of her class from Stanford Law School but couldn't get a job. After having three sons she went back to work 15 years later and eventually became the first female Justice on Supreme Court in the US.

"From a personal point of view you need to realize your potential, and if you don't you will be an unhappy person," Johnson adds. "As a woman, as a professional, dig deep and find those strengths and have the courage to have other people realize that potential – make it public." Her advice for women who aren't getting what they need from work? "A lesson I learned from my father: you have to ask."

Jude Kelly, Artistic Director, Southbank Centre, UK

Jude Kelly's approach to a barrier is to find a way around it, having grown up in a family of four daughters, with a father who championed each of them in whatever they wanted to do. Jude recognizes the immense power of this environment in shaping her personality and ambition: "I was the kind of person who tried to do things, got things done, wasn't going to take no for an answer, all of that. There is something about never being in a situation where you are made to feel second place. However, I should add that my father was adamant that this was not because WE were especially entitled. He believed in everyone's potential, however unlikely their backgrounds might be."

This foundation provided a strong base for Jude when she did hit barriers at university: "I had university lecturers who were very doubting and very sexist. The effect it had on me was to make me more determined, and this is an issue, isn't it? About what impact somebody's negativity has on you. And what support structures you have."

These shaped Jude's aspirations and her sense of social purpose. She realized working in the arts was a means to create "wider cultural democracy," involve more people by "including everybody in the world of the arts, and therefore speaking with the world. And once I had understood how strongly I felt about that, then in a sense you have something other than just your own desire for yourself to apply your ambition to."

From the beginning of her career, Jude looked for challenging opportunities, even if this meant stretching her profile. "Well, a little story was lying about my age because I went for an interview for a director when I was 22 and they laughed, when I told them my age, they didn't exactly say you're such a young woman, what do you mean, but there was that kind of attitude. And so my next interview I said I was 24, I might have got the job anyway but then I was in a state of anguish for several years hoping they wouldn't find out my age. That was a risk based on the fact that I was assessing whether I could be taken seriously."

Jude acknowledged the power of champions who have supported the development of her career, and in particular men in senior roles who recognized her potential and supported her by absolute belief in her capabilities. "I had fantastic men who did champion women who themselves knew that sexism existed. And it's seen as paternalistic, I mean they weren't paternalistic, they were kindly, which is not the same thing. So a string of tremendous men, that's the first thing. I remember that much more than I remember women championing me. And that's not because women didn't champion me, because women weren't in position so they couldn't. They weren't there." Recognizing this gap in the support system for women has led to Jude stepping up as a champion but also arguing her focus is firmly on promoting talent: "I mean I've always championed women, employed them, I think not exclusively but most of the young directors that I trained were women."

Society still has a long way to go, argues Jude: "We're still living in a society where male endorsement is still seen as more legitimate," and there is greater pressure on women to achieve "wanting it all" and "that begins with the narrative that it is women who will be the primary carers of children. And then that suggests that everything else is additional – and personal ambition – almost as if it's a luxury – and so it produces immediately anxiety about can you do all those things, should you do all these things, and the word 'selfish' is applied to women by others and themselves in a way men rarely experience."

In spite of these challenges, Jude is optimistic about the future but she describes how women need to change their attitudes to maintain the momentum; they need to be bolder about asking for equality at all times as their human right: "Women can find themselves being taken for granted and overlooked and underestimated because they think that people will notice what they're doing or spot their potential, but the evidence is the opposite. People don't advance or promote you unless you make it really clear that that's what you want. So a lot of women have tried to avoid looking ambitious and then simply not being acknowledged and it's led to them feeling bitter and disappointed. We have to realize that ambition is not a dirty word. Gaining influence allows you to do more good for others so it's worth having for that reason."

Hannah Kimuyu, Director, Greenlight Digital Marketing, UK

"I might have benefited from initiatives to support gender or race diversity, but if I did I didn't recognize them. I've had three jobs: in Capital One I had a female manager and a female team around me, in Energy Savings Trust the same, and in Greenlight my original boss was also female, so it was never an issue."

From being a level-headed, astute teenager, who at 19, and in her first role during a gap year from university, devised a unique government information-sharing intranet, it was evident Hannah was going to be a success story. Fast forward to the present, at 36-years-old she is a young director. Interestingly, her path has not been paved with the challenges we have heard of from other women in leadership. Hers is one of resilience, dedication, and a relatively smooth transition. Where Hannah did face obstacles was when the autonomy and promotion she craved, and knew she was heading for, came too slowly. "I always knew I wanted to be a leader – I don't know why, perhaps because I was always popular at school ... I am full of confidence – perhaps too confident and never afraid to put myself out there."

Hannah's three jobs have given her all the exposure needed to further her career in her chosen field of communications. From brand management and online marketing at Capital One to the Energy Savings Trust, where she immersed herself in her role as New Media Executive with responsibility for search engine optimization and management, together with a budget of £1.1 million. She realized there was great potential in this kind of marketing, which had not yet been explored because they just did not know enough about it, and it was growing at a phenomenal rate. Hannah eventually secured a position at Greenlight, which looked upon her budget experience most favorably. She was taken on as part of a two-person team reporting to one of the owners, who was also a woman. Consequently, she was given the autonomy she craved and managed half of the portfolio of accounts right away.

This was her best career move yet, for within six months Hannah was promoted and she recruited a team of her own staff. She had made a point of keeping up with her networks and staying friends with staff, even those who moved on to rival agencies.

Greenlight grew rapidly, moving offices several times. With some large client contracts, the agency doubled in size and moved to a more traditional corporate environment with glass walls, an atrium, and individual offices for managers, completely changing the nature of the company. During this expansion it was a new recruit, Natalie, who became pivotal in Hannah's journey. Her influence was around enabling Hannah to find herself as a woman and to appreciate her privileged route to becoming a director. Although Natalie eventually moved on to a position at a women's charity, the Women's Resource Centre where Hannah is also Chair on the Board, the pair remained best friends.

Prompted to consider who has shaped her life, Hannah replies, "My mother was definitely one major influence, the other is Natalie. Natalie said to me that I did not encounter difficulties." And about barriers for women entering leadership roles she responds, "Barriers? I don't see barriers. Of course I am a feminist, but I don't use that label, don't call myself that, because I am not educated in feminism. In my job I know my stuff so I don't want to claim expertise where I don't have it." Regarding initiatives to support gender diversity, Hannah is encouraging, "Greenlight wants to see more females at the top so are trying to push the issue internally and encourage those capable. We have people from all countries and all nationalities – color doesn't come into the mix – we are a young industry, I am a director at 36."

As for advice that she does feel qualified to give, Hannah is again plainly honest, "The difference for me was to change from being a manager to being a leader. As a leader you need to absorb the negativity before you can solve it and use that to change it for yourself and the team. You do have a personal cost as a leader – in your work–life balance and your relationships. I always hired people smarter than me so I could hand things over and go forward. And don't hang onto things too much. The rewards for me are financial and what I can do with that for others."

Aliza Knox, Managing Director Online Sales, Twitter, APAC, and LATAM (Singapore)

Aliza Knox is someone whose career has been guided by creating and seizing opportunities. She stretched herself by seeking out roles that seemed exciting, with curiosity being one of the main drivers. Having grown up and worked in the US until her mid-20s, Aliza decided she wanted to experience life in another country. "Having been told I didn't have the language skills to work in Asia, and having suffered through six months of damp and cold during a semester abroad in England, I applied for a job in Australia. I knew no one there and knew nothing about business 'down under.'" She took a big risk moving to a new country in a new role simultaneously.

It turned out Aliza really liked Australia and her job at the Boston Consulting Group (BCG). She stuck with both for some time. After making partner, she was finally given the chance to move to Asia; she went to Singapore to build BCG's financial services practice there. An approach from a US corporate that wanted to create an international presence persuaded her to move her family back to the US. Again, she was driven by the excitement of the role and the ability to build something.

She returned to the US and delivered strong results for financial services companies Schwab and Visa. A chance business meeting with a Google senior executive got her thinking about trying another "new thing."

Aliza started over in a new industry, taking a title and pay cut to be part of the tech world in Silicon Valley. "I'm an opportunist and was more excited by the challenge than concerned about my title." She moved back to Asia for Google and subsequently joined Twitter in Singapore as Managing Director, Online Sales, APAC and LATAM.

Aliza also holds three non-executive director positions. She is the only woman on the Singapore Post board (10 per cent owned by Alibaba). She also sits on the boards of GfK (market research, Germany), and Scentre Group (shopping malls, Australia).

Her unique combination of expertise in financial services and digital media, as well as her proven track record as an executive, have made her a sought-after candidate for boards.

How has being a woman impacted her career? She asserts that she'll never know for sure. In some cases, it may have made things tougher. On the other hand, she has experienced strong support at times. While at BCG, a client asked to have her removed from their project upon finding out she was pregnant. Her male colleague reminded the client that they had asked for the best project leader and suggested if they still wanted this, they should keep Aliza on – and they did.

Aliza has a strong interest in diversity of all sorts, including gender. She believes a mixture of backgrounds and perspectives on teams and in companies generates better results and a more interesting work environment. She says, "I benefit from working on diversity issues. I find it personally fulfilling. It is something I believe in and feel good about. I often get to work with younger women to help them develop and advance." Even when budgets were tight, Aliza found a way to create opportunities for women to build their own networks and identify different career options, something she felt was crucial for younger women who were unaware of obstacles they might face later on. "When you are 25 and working at many of today's MNCs where 50 per cent of the incoming hires are women, you may think women no longer face any issues." While she hopes that will be true for most of them, she wants them to have the confidence, perspective, and infrastructure to tackle challenges – especially gender-related ones – as they arise.

Aliza's extensive travel and experiences have provided her with a broad perspective on the position of women in the workplace. She still sees a lot of barriers due to social pressures on women once they get married and have children in a number of Asian countries.

In addition, there are challenges around how women lead: "Women are expected to behave in different ways that no one can quite quantify." There have been numerous articles on this topic recently, including a series by Adam Grant and Sheryl Sandberg, relating to how women are perceived and evaluated differently from men when exhibiting similar behavior.

Aliza has a strong commitment to maintaining support for women, and describes the benefits of having advocates. "There's always more than one person for a job or a board seat. An advocate is someone willing to stick their neck out for you." Particularly in areas where they are under-represented, such as in senior management or on boards, women benefit from having someone advocate on their behalf. This is where women who have reached certain milestones can help other women by suggesting their names or reinforcing their competence. Aliza regularly champions women into board roles; "paying it forward" is something she believes in and practices.

What else will be in her leadership legacy? Role-modeling courage (or is it craziness?), and the value in building a career based on what is exciting: "I took on jobs that sounded fun and challenging I wanted to build businesses and deliver results. I've been told I've had a 'non-linear' career, but I'm happy with that. I encourage other women to let their curiosity and interests drive their decision-making, instead of relying exclusively on pay or title. I'm convinced this leads to greater work satisfaction."

Catherine Lesetedi-Letegele, CEO Botswana Life Insurance, Botswana

Catherine's career trajectory does not exactly suggest someone who has found it hard to overcome problems. She worked for the Botswana government for a year after a degree in statistics and demography, but soon decided that she was entrepreneurial by nature and moved into the insurance industry. Having worked for large Botswana insurance firms IGI and AON, by 2006 she was Assistant General Manager of Botswana Life and then became CEO, turning it into the leader in the life insurance industry with 80 per cent of the domestic market.

In her five years in the top job, she has introduced numerous innovations. For example, seeing the potential of mobile phones, she set up a mobile payment platform for people to pay their premiums through their phones. More recently, she launched the Life Rewards card, a prepaid Visa card the firm gives to customers when paying out claims, which gives them discounts at certain retailers – the only scheme of its type in Sub-Saharan Africa outside of South Africa.

She was helped in her career by one man in particular – a manager at IGI encouraged her, then recruited her as his successor at AON later, and, "many years later he encouraged me to take a role when I was headhunted." However, she says that she was once held back by a male boss. "He overlooked me for a long time, he just did not have time for women," she says. His successor – also a man – "only looked at talent and promoted me twice in a year," saying that he "could not understand why I was at such a low level." Even now, on a daily basis, she says, she comes across men who "underestimate you" as a woman. "You come across these undertones, but I am able to work around them."

She says that taking on the CEO role at BLIL was a risk, but "more for the shareholders than me. I had no track record of prior experience of running an organization." An added difficulty is that she took the role at the height of the global economic downturn. But things have worked out well. She credits her "networking skills, and logical problem-solving skills" with helping her to double the business's assets, and give a return on embedded value that is way above expectations. The business is now also "much more innovative and entrepreneurial in approach," she says.

Has anyone inspired her? Her father, she says, was her first role model. "He encouraged me a lot, even though he was not highly educated." Another inspirational figure was Wendy Luhabe, a South African entrepreneur who created Women Investment Portfolio Holdings – a fund that allowed 18,000 women to become investors for the first time – and also launched a fund to provide capital to female-run businesses. Linah Mohohlo, the Governor of the Bank of Botswana is also a role model.

Catherine is very keen to ensure that leadership is seen in a broad sense, and has set up a voluntary group at BLIL which supports primary schools, for instance by giving them stationery. "I want to be exemplary beyond the corporate sphere," she says, "and give an example of being able to give. This also creates an awareness of what a whole leader can be, and using that as a positive model both inside and outside the workplace." She also coaches female graduates – and recently took on a male one for the first time.

What would she say to the next generation of female leaders? "The greatest lesson I can teach them is to be your authentic self," says Catherine. "The best person you can be is yourself, so be self-forgiving, be open to new ideas, network with like-minded individuals, most of all accept your imperfections and leverage your strengths. She goes on to say, "Women need to work together to create networks through which they can collaborate. We need to make an extra effort to connect with other women. We need to be in the spotlight, and emphasize the importance and benefits of networks."

She believes that women sometimes create their own barriers. "As women, we tend to take on too much. Early on, you need to know what you want and the kind of leader you want to be," she says. "You need to create a support structure around yourself at home and at work to achieve what you want. For example, my husband supports me and is not worried or annoyed if I have to work until 11 at night to finish a project. You need a support structure so that if a child is sick it is not automatically you, the woman, who has to take time off to take the child to a clinic, as society dictates. If you can share that with your partner, you can progress your career as well."

Younger women, she thinks, are ambitious, but also need to be realistic. "I think the younger generation is more aware of the benefit of having mentors and coaches," she says. "But sometimes they are impatient, and I want to tell them to slow down. It takes time to get to where I am now."

Parveen Mahmud, Managing Director, Grameen Telecom Trust, Bangladesh

How many times do you say no to a Nobel Prize winner? Parveen Mahmud has the distinct record of not only saying no twice to a distinguished prize winner, but when she finally did say yes, she still made him wait for her. Parveen has a track record of breaking barriers and achieving firsts throughout her professional career, culminating in her current role as the first Managing Director of the newly launched Grameen Telecom Trust – appointed by Professor Mohamed Yunus, Nobel Peace Laureate, 2006, founder, Grameen Bank, Initiator of Social Business Concept and Chairman, Grameen Telecom Trust.

Her career started when Parveen, aged 18, moved to the UK with her husband, who was teaching economics and was studying barrister-at-law. Parveen finished her education and began her studies to be a chartered accountant. Family needs recalled her to Bangladesh and during that time, while she was taking care of her mother-in-law, she became mother of two children, so she took a career break for seven years. Later on, in 1982, she resumed her studies and carried out her articleship with a chartered accountant's firm in Dhaka, Bangladesh. Her husband, who had previously been very active in sharing childcare responsibilities, had been appointed as a government minister and was unable to maintain that support and so she left the firm, finishing the mandatory required articleship to be a chartered accountant, and stopped working.

Parveen started her career with BRAC in 1991 and moved on to ActionAid Bangladesh as Financial Controller. She was the only female financial controller in AAB's country programs at that point of time in 1994–95. In ActionAid her career was progressing well, but a year later Parveen turned down an international assignment and left the AAB job due to family considerations. She always wanted to pursue a career in the development sector. But in this sector, frequent travel on field trips is expected and for her to manage that was difficult with two small children.

From 1996 she joined ACNABIN, a chartered accountancy firm and became partner. When her children went to university, Parveen reignited and diversified her career with a long-cherished desire to contribute to the development of Bangladesh. In late 1999, she started working for a government-sponsored, not-for-profit company, Palli Karma-Sahayak Foundation (PKSF) as a full-time adviser. PKSF is an institution working in wholesaling funds for microfinance to Microfinance Institutes (MFIs) and institutions working towards employment creation and poverty alleviation. Later, she became Deputy Managing Director.

In 2007, Parveen became the first female council member for the Institute of Chartered Accountants of Bangladesh (ICAB), and served two terms in this role. Following this, she was elected first female Vice President (2008) and was elected as the first female President in 2011. She was also the first female board member of the South Asian Federation of Accountants (SAFA) in 2011.

During her tenure as President of ICAB, she was offered the role of MD for Grameen Telecom Trust by Professor Yunus, who was a board member of PKSF. He provided flexibility for the role, but Parveen was clear she couldn't leave her presidency unfinished. He offered her the chance to work with him part-time and again she refused. Although her role as President was an honorary role, she resigned from PKSF and dedicated full-time to the ICAB, as she wanted to fulfill her commitments at ICAB, bringing in positive changes, so he agreed to wait until she finished her presidency before appointing her in May, 2012. Parveen has a passion for working with social business innovations to bring positive changes in lives, communities, and society as a whole for a sustainable world.

Parveen was Working Group Member for the Consultative Group on Social Indicators, UNCTAD/ISAR. She serves on various boards, working for social causes, and was the Chairperson for the Acid Survivors Foundation. Parveen was a member of the National Advisory Panel for SME Development of Bangladesh and founding board member of the SME Foundation. She was also

Convener of the SME Women's Forum. She serves on various boards, including BRAC International, ActionAid International Bangladesh, MIDAS, Manusher Jannyo Foundation (MJF), and the Under Privileged Children Educational Program (UCEP) in Bangladesh. She is the Chairperson of Shasha Denims Limited and the Shasha Foundation. She has sponsored "President 2011 – Shasha Scholarship" for two ICAB female students studying chartered accountancy. She also received the Begum Rokeya Shining Personality Award 2006 for women's empowerment from the Narikantha Foundation.

As Parveen shares her experiences of working at senior levels, it is clear that she has continuously challenged the status quo and that she draws on her own experiences managing family and work in viewing the organizational culture and structure. Her leadership is embedded in doing what is right and she has no hesitation in speaking up. This is a trait she developed from the earliest stages in her career, challenging expenses even on relative minor items that were not approved within a charity. "I am not afraid to bring things up to the higher management, to speak the truth and find out the right things. I think they appreciated this." She believes in ensuring transparency and accountability. To ensure good governance she was never hesitant. When she suspected a non-transparent transaction had taken place in a project land purchase deal, she was not afraid to launch an investigation. She travelled to the remote village and revealed the irregularities.

Her strong sense of justice means she has continuously challenged behavior that is not aligned to the values of the organizations she works for: "One of my support staff suddenly had an accident and died on the spot. He had a young wife and a small baby. I went out of my way to help the family with office benefits. At that time, I found myself in a male-dominated environment, everybody was against the situation. I was surprised. They were not sympathetic to the wife, they wanted me to hand out benefits to the mother or brother and not to the wife! I took my decision with the Country Director after consulting the lawyer. Within 40 days I had helped the young wife to learn to sign, because she was not educated, and to get control of her life. I helped her to get the majority of the funds which will help her to raise her child."

Her strong sense of justice comes from her family, and in particular the women in her family. Her maternal grandmother had a strong commitment to the welfare of the neighborhood. She says her mother had inspiring leadership qualities: "My mother got married very early at 15 years. She studied privately for the school-leaving SSC exam and then she studied HSC in college, when she had four children, and successfully graduated. She was a pioneer in social work and an exemplary lady in the development sector – not only in Chittagong but also in Bangladesh. In 1978, she founded Ghashful, the first registered NGO in Chittagong. She was an outstanding lady who dedicated her life for the betterment of slum dwellers of Chittagong, Dalit (untouchable communities), for education of underprivileged children, for health, and for women's empowerment. She has received awards and recognition for her dedication as social entrepreneur and travelled quite extensively." Her experiences were shared with other senior women in her network: they all had similar experiences around the glass ceiling and challenges in managing their personal and work responsibilities. "In my personal life I have found it has not been that easy, when giving a senior position to a woman. So, being in senior position, I always tried and fought to recruit women in higher key positions and to help women in roles with higher authority." Parveen considers herself lucky to have reached a level where she has authority, so she is committed to inspiring other women to move up the ladder.

Puan Sri Maimon, Malaysian Mosaics, Malaysia

"I'm a passionate learner and I am grateful for the ability to get into a role," states Puan Sri Maimon. This is evidenced by her wide range of roles at Malaysian Mosaics (MMSB). Since joining in 1991, she has worked in several departments, including marketing services, communications, managing the design team, corporate liaison, technical research and development, new product development, and quality management. She is currently a director and Head of Quality for MMSB. She has set up a corporate social responsibility (CSR) department for the Hap Seng group, a conglomerate with common majority shareholder as MMSB. "Looking back over my career with this company, I realize I have been assigned to set up new departments and transferred to do something else; that seems to be an area where I gravitate." She previously set up Mosaic's marketing services department from scratch.

"The skills I developed with setting up departments were helpful when I moved to the corporate office," she says. "In the corporate office, the art of persuasion and getting the buy-in from the chief executives is very important. As a CSR director, my role is to provoke the CSR conversation. "I was trained and now it is ingrained in me to manage by provocation," she says. "In MMSB, I am surrounded by a lot of men – ceramics and manufacturing are masculine industries. For many years, when we travelled overseas, I was the only woman. Also, earlier in my career I spent five years in property development and the construction industry, which was also a very masculine environment."

Several champions helped her progress, including the CEO at MMSB when she joined, who "believed in management by provocation. He always provoked me to move to the next level." More recently, her COO championed her as he "believed in me more than I believed in myself and opened up the possibility of this corporate role."

What are the barriers that stop women moving into leadership roles? "This is a question I have never asked myself because for me it has never been about gender," she says. "But now as I am exposed to the Women on Boards program, I start to ask my men friends who are on public listed boards, 'Why don't you allow more women onto the board?' When I look at my peers I realize that women tend to not ask, whereas men do negotiate their way up. It's about getting yourself heard."

She had never benefited from any gender program and says that "I didn't really believe in gender programs until I went on the Board program. I had never been involved in any gender groups. I remember sitting in the program and feeling very uncomfortable when everyone was talking about women issues. I am always in an environment where gender has never been an issue."

Working at board level has also opened her eyes to the power her championing could have. "I was telling a group of women that it may not be possible for all of us to sit on the board," she says. "I am not that optimistic, but by having this conversation it opens up the door and the possibility for women of the next generation, to make it easier for them to go into that area. It creates confidence for women of the next generation to move to the next level of thinking."

She has also championed women to move into roles, assuaging middle-management's worries about promoting certain women. "Management felt they weren't ready, but I said I would 'hold their hand' for a year and if they didn't step up, then they can bring in a new person." This has, almost always, been a success. "I have also gone to the extent of identifying high potentials and sending them to awareness courses," she adds. "Once they become aware of their potential, there is a chance they will leave, and two of them did – one of whom became a successful entrepreneur."

Women can limit themselves, Maimon thinks, by being content with their jobs and lacking ambition. "When men are good at something, the normal course of action will be to look for promotion," she says. "A lot of women grow into their role and become happy to stay in it and they become a limiting person."

"I always tell my colleagues, my job is to get me out of this job and your job is to make sure you can get into my job," she says. "The thinking needs to be there from day one. I suppose that is one of the reasons that allows me to move around. I am always challenged by the learning."

Nurjehan Mawani C. M., Aga Khan Development Network, Diplomatic (AKDN) Representative for Afghanistan

Nurjehan Mawani C.M. is a member of the Order of Canada having been conferred an award by the Governor General in recognition of her contribution to public service and work with women refugees.

"Self-realization is part of every human being's aspiration and responsibility. Often it gets diminished because circumstances are just so difficult. However, if you come from the premise that everyone has a spark, and despite the severity of the challenges, there is a spark which can be ignited. We as individuals have a sense of responsibility; we can't say, 'Oh it's too big. I can't do anything.'" Nurjehan stays true to her humanistic roots, and from the very start of her career as a lawyer in the UK, she combined a successful legal practice with volunteerism to assist the plight of refugees coming out of Uganda. Soon after moving to Canada, her career took an interesting turn. She was appointed to the Immigration Appeal Board as a result of her voluntary work in immigration – born of her dedication and desire to help those less fortunate. She says of her voluntary experience, "it was inspired by the underlying ethics emanating strongly from the community, one of self-help and helping others – a humanistic approach." Nurjehan notes poignantly that she owes much to the synchronicity and meshing of her professional life and her volunteering work. "I don't believe we pay enough attention as to how our voluntary and professional careers can be mutually reinforcing. This has been a pattern for me all the way back to my school days and through my entire life."

Nurjehan continued her commitment to volunteerism whilst raising her two young children, with a supportive husband who was also finding his way in a new country, and the dedication of her recently widowed mother. As an immigrant herself, she was all too aware that she needed to forge connections beyond the familiar and stay grounded. "During this time I reached out beyond the comfort zone of my community and joined other networks, for example Science World, which created new opportunities for board roles, new thinking, and new contacts. As a new immigrant, I felt it was very important to get involved in mainstream organizations and reach out, and in so doing, opened a path for others."

Known for the quality of her work, her ethics, and characteristics, Nurjehan found herself propelled into a senior role and eventually made it to the biggest platform of her career. Nurjehan was the very first new Canadian to be appointed by the Prime Minister as the Chairperson and Chief Executive Officer of Canada's largest tribunal, the Immigration and Refugee Board (IRB). "I believe I had established a track record. What is interesting is that the legislation was changed from chairman to chairperson, symbolizing Canadian values of inclusion. At the same time, the legislation created the concept of chairperson's guidelines. These guidelines enabled me to deal with new challenges that were emerging in a complex environment. The very first influx of Afghan refugee claimants arrived when I was the Chair and CEO of the IRB. I feel all of these experiences were building blocks to the position I currently hold." The role of chairperson of IRB was a huge stretch for Nurjehan, which to her credit she carried out with aplomb. Balancing the complexity of the relationship with various stakeholders – including ministers, parliament, UNHCR, NGOs, academia, and media – was no mean feat. Not content with an already challenging assignment, Nurjehan also brought the gender issue to the forefront. "As the chairperson, I had the authority to issue guidelines, and saw a compelling reason to recognize gender-related persecution within the refugee convention. To do this, it took 'institutional imagination', and building a community of support around a groundbreaking initiative, all the while within the requirement of the law. And as in many such initiatives, there was a risk of non-acceptance: there was pushback but there was also support, which had to be built widely and deeply, step by step."

Nurjehan speaks candidly about being authentic, how one's inner and outer selves need to be in alignment so that there is harmony between principle and action: "You have to believe in something yourself. If you don't believe in it you won't be authentic." In her current role in Afghanistan with the Aga Khan Development Network, she works tirelessly to promote women's and girls' education and economic empowerment – in what is a complex and conservative environment. "There is a strong appetite and desire to learn. Women are highly motivated and it's incredible to see the extent of their commitment and resilience. At the recent London Conference on Afghanistan, His Highness the Aga Khan noted, 'Women's participation in society is vital to ensure an improved quality of life. From education to health, participation in local governance to leadership in business, we have witnessed the potential for women and men to work alongside each other, while respecting the ethics of Islam, to build their communities.'"

Nurjehan is passionately committed to consolidating the gains that have been made with respect to women's changing roles in the region, working with like-minded partners and stakeholders and the women themselves. She has an admirable record in influencing changes in attitude, often having to win over resistance born out of fear or ignorance. Needless to say, these have been overcome by embracing the very spirit Nurjehan advocates. "We need to build on a model of leadership that leverages the strengths of female leadership. If you unpack that model, what are the differences, and why is this going to be critically different for the world we live in. Women and children are the biggest victims during conflict but are never at the table when peace is negotiated, there is a big disconnect there." Of barriers faced by women in leadership roles, she says this: "I think women need more champions: There is an important distinction between a sponsor and a champion. A sponsor may not have alignment with goals, but sees you as someone who can help to achieve what they want to achieve. Championing is about genuine alignment and igniting the spark."

Maria Msiska, Managing Director, BOC Kenya

An accountant by training, early in her career Maria Msiska found herself working as a lecturer at the University of Malawi, but decided that academic life was not for her. She got a job at Coopers and Lybrand in Malawi. At the time, she stood out. "In the late 1980s in Malawi there weren't many female auditors," she says. "I remember when I went to help a colleague because he was behind schedule with the audit, the client addressed me as a stenographer. It was very difficult for the client to accept that there were female auditors."

However, she was given responsibility and male mentors helped her. "My first assignment was secondment to a client company," she remembers. "Even though I had little prior management experience, my boss walked me through the process." She ran the business for three months. A stint working in the UK followed, but her big break, when she returned to Malawi, was to be headhunted to join Industrial Gases in 1994. She quickly rose to be Managing Director – the first female MD in the group in the region. She was transferred to Zambia, then to South Africa as Head of Finance for several countries, and then finally transferred to Kenya as Managing Director with responsibility for East Africa.

Champions have been important in her rise. "I've been very lucky, in that the bosses I've worked for have been great mentors and have given me a lot of support with my work. They have helped me to climb the career ladder," she says.

Msiska says that she tries to recruit women, but that "I feel that there are times when women do not always understand how demanding the role they are being recruited for is. And for some of them it is not always easy to decide on prioritization and balance between work and family. In this part of the world if you take on a woman in a senior role, if the child gets sick the domestic responsibilities still kick in. If not well managed, you end up missing important deadlines."

One problem is a lack of legal support for working women. "One of my former bosses once told me: 'I am taking you on but I am treating you just like any other manager,'" she remembers. "As the other managers were all male at the time, I later understood this to mean that I would get no maternity leave. There was no law governing such benefits at the time. I always remind women that if you want to pursue a career working for someone you need to sort out your priorities in advance, and understand the demands of the role upfront to avoid disappointment."

Msiska thinks that women sometimes don't grasp their chances. "Women sometimes feel they are not getting the right opportunities to get into senior positions, they don't get big business opportunities as entrepreneurs," she says. "I was at a function once where older women said to younger women: 'We have fought a lot for you and have broken male dominance in the work place. Your problem is you are not networking with the right people. When you see an opportunity you don't go for it.' And I think they are right. Women sometimes don't network with the right people. The opportunities are there, it's how they view these opportunities and how they go after them that could be a hindrance."

For example, women sometimes absorb cultural preconceptions. "There is still a general belief that certain jobs are not for women, and unfortunately sometimes women themselves believe it too," she says. "In a male-dominated industry there is a tendency to recruit men for certain positions, but this may be due to the fact that capable women do not always apply for these positions. And unfortunately if women do not grab the opportunity to apply, they will have locked themselves out. It's where we've come from that's holding women back."

How can women be encouraged in sub-Saharan Africa? "We need more mentors for women. The other day I was pleasantly surprised to hear someone refer to me as their role model. I believe that's my impact." During her career, she says, she has helped several people from the organizations she has worked for as well as other organizations. "I was prepared to hand-hold them until they became fully confident in their management roles."

Encouraging more organizations to employ women could have a huge impact on her region, thinks Msiska. "If you employ a woman, she invariably makes sure her children are looked after by providing for their basic needs in life," she says. "It's very important that women access opportunities to better their lives and those of their families. There cannot be meaningful development without the involvement of women. Women, particularly those in rural areas, need to be encouraged to access opportunities. There must be deliberate efforts to bring these women into the workforce where possible and they should be supported through appropriate policies and structures in order to reach their full potential. This will not only help reduce poverty levels but will also improve literacy levels."

She adds, "I would like to encourage more women to aim higher."

Jan Owen, CEO, Foundation for Young Australians, Australia

"I have always had a strong entrepreneurial drive," says Jan Owen. "As a child, I set up a lemonade stand on a road that maybe saw five cars go by a week. I was deeply optimistic that I could create and sell even if there were no customers." The lemonade stall might not have made her a fortune, but it taught her skills that she soon put to good use. Aged just 16, she set up Australia's first motor mechanics course in a girls' school. But rather than go on to build businesses, she became a social entrepreneur, creating new solutions to societal problems. She was no doubt set on that track by her family, which, she says, "was very community minded," and helped establish Lifeline, the first phone counselling service in Australia.

Although she didn't flourish academically ("Education failed me, I didn't fail it"), she was a born leader, and excelled at debating and sport, and wrote the school newsletter. "I was entrepreneurial, inspired and motivated others," she says. Time spent in the UK as a child (where her father, an academic, worked for a while) also broadened her horizons, as did travelling to China as a youth leader on an Australian diplomatic mission when she was 22. As soon as she could, she left school, tried university three times, and studied part-time until she found her calling, doing youth work, mainly with Aboriginal and Torres Strait islander children and young people on the inner city streets of Brisbane. "I didn't ask permission to do new things, I just asked forgiveness later. We would take over service stations that had gone out of business and create drop-in centers, and then write to Shell to ask for permission – we were always looking for smart, entrepreneurial ways of doing things," she remembers.

Her experiences working in child protection spurred her to set up the CREATE Foundation, the first national consumer organization for children and young people in foster care. This was a somewhat revolutionary organization. "I had been nominated for a national role in youth policy and realized that systemic change was very important and that I needed to be strategically disruptive," she says.

Soon after, Owen was awarded a 12-month fellowship to the Peter Drucker Foundation in the US and learned about social impact and venture philanthropy. "In Australia, we sometimes felt we were a bit of a 'backwater,' but after that experience I felt we could completely hold our own. I had the sense that at CREATE we were actually ahead of the game," she says. "It gave me a real ambition and drive to create social change." She also saw the benefits that Australia offered: "In order to access funds and influence, you need to know the right people. And there are only three degrees of separation in Australia compared to six in other more heavily populated countries," she says.

She went on to help establish Social Ventures Australia (SVA), based on the US model of Venture Philanthropy, with Michael Traill, a former investment banker from Macquarie Bank. They raised AU$26 million in three years and SVA became a key non-profit consultancy and impact investor in social enterprise. When private childcare provider ABC Learning went into administration, SVA led a consortium of charities to turn it into a social enterprise, Goodstart, with 650 centers and 150 linked businesses. It became one of the largest social enterprises in the world.

In 2011, Owen was asked to run the largest independent foundation working for young people in Australia; a role that utilizes her social enterprise skills and non-profit experience. FYA inspires, equips, and backs a generation of young change agents and social entrepreneurs, aged 12 to 28.

Although she never benefited from initiatives to support women – "they didn't exist when I was starting out or through-out my career in the social sector" – Owen identifies many role models as guides, including one of Australia's first female clergy ("a very strong, determined woman!"); Dame Quentin Bryce, Australia's first female Governor-General; Michael Traill, co-founder of Macquarie direct investment; Peter Drucker; and "many young people in care, who were really smart, with drive and passion."

She has always tried to champion women during her career: "I've often built strong female teams and women have come to work for me because I am known as a female leader," she says. "I have always promoted women and supported families – and that is the key enabler for women. I am a mother and foster mother, and a conscious backer of women, especially young women." She goes on to say, "I have a large group of young people whom I actively sponsor, both male and female. I am also a big believer in 'reverse mentoring' and have a number of under-30-year-olds who mentor me. I find two-way mentoring the most powerful and enriching."

Owen continues, "I see the next generation of social entre-preneurs and leaders as extremely driven, highly skilled and very powerful, more so than in my generation. Today managers, architects, engineers, landscapers, people from diverse backgrounds are involved in social change." She believes that women can be the most effective catalysts for change. "Women invest in the next generation," she says. "They have the ability to be mission critical and at the same time aware of their emotional wake. Women leaders often have unique capabilities to convene, collaborate, and bring people along with them. If you want innovation and disruption, it will come from the next generation. And young women are very much up for that."

Robyn Joy Pratt, Owner-Director, Impact Consulting, Malta

"Looking back, I wonder how I did it," says Robyn Pratt, who has enjoyed a hugely successful career spanning three countries. A clue might be in her upbringing on a farm in Queensland in Australia with two strong female role models. "My grandmother and mother were active in the Australian Countrywomen's Association, making contributions to helping women in the countryside," she says. Her mother, she adds, "always wanted to be more independent than she could be living on a farm." Her grandmother's example was also evidently formative. "My mother died at 58, but my grandmother remained very much part of our lives and someone who I very much admired as I entered a pivotal time in my career. She was always very interested in what we were all doing and loved to share news of the lives of her many grandchildren and great-grandchildren. She kept the tribe together, which in a way is important when we consider effective leadership in this day and age. Keeping the team engaged and inspired is an important element of successful leadership," says Robyn.

Hard work was another trait Robyn inherited. Aged 21, she owned her own restaurant. She won a business woman of the year competition, sponsored by a hotel chain who then offered her a job. By 25 she had moved into marketing and although her boss was charismatic, he was quite traditional in his thinking. "He told me that he believed that a woman's place was in the home and that I should consider this and not be so ambitious," says Robyn. "This was like waving a red rag to a bull and made me even more determined." She became a general manager with Starwood, and went on to work for 23 years with the company in various positions, "and I believe I was one of the youngest and very few female GMs at that time."

Combining the motherhood duties of a family of three boys with her career was not always straightforward. "As a single mother, there were times when I had to leave my middle son as a baby to housekeeping or in the kitchen when I had to meet with a guest. A hotel GM job is a 24-hour position and as I did not have family close by, there was no alternative." Robyn had the opportunity to relocate to Brussels with Starwood. It was a difficult decision to leave her family but she decided to take up the offer and with her partner, who is now her husband, began her career with Starwood EMEA office, moving through various leadership positions in quality and brand leadership for 240 hotels across the region. In 2010, they made the decision to move to Malta, due to a position offered to her husband with a Malta-based hotel company.

The move from Australia to Europe was not an easy one. "It is not easy going from being a big fish in a small sea to a small fish in a big sea and I was feeling very sorry for myself," Robyn says. But a fellow Australian woman coached her through the transition: "She taught me that feeling sorry for yourself isn't the answer and if you want something then you have to prove yourself and your value." She learned that establishing credibility and trust is crucial when going into any new challenge.

Robyn says that she has never benefited from any formal scheme to help women, which is "why I want to become more involved in coaching and mentoring women for leadership positions, more like coaching." She has coached various people who have worked for her into leadership roles, including women. "To be honest, I don't consider gender when agreeing to help develop someone – everyone is entitled to aspire to achieve the best they can do. What I do find is that when coaching or mentoring women, a lot more time is taken to discuss how to balance role of wife or mother with a career – particularly one which involves leadership and managing others."

She thinks that job-sharing and flexible working would help women progress, and in general "a recognition that women – and men – do have to balance childcare and work and to help support this in the workplace." The best thing we can do for the next generation of leaders, both female and male, says Robyn is to "share our own experiences" with young people. Mentors should "provide our expertise and insights but understand that how this will be implemented may need to be different now, because of how the world has changed, for example the introduction of technology which was not there when I was moving through my career."

She thinks there needs to be more focus on diversity in leadership because it leads to "happier employees, better understanding with customers, and in the long-term better bottom line results." Companies need to balance the business: "One without the other will create challenges, especially in relation to effective leadership. These days it is vital to consider the importance of emotional intelligence in leading people, just as much as the academic and experience aspect. Research has proven that one without the other will not be as effective."

Rt. Hon. Dame Jenny Shipley, former Prime Minister, New Zealand

A champion of champions is the most appropriate title for Dame Jenny Shipley. The former Prime Minister of New Zealand displays the impact of having a clear vision and leading with "intent" and being very clear on the end result.

Dame Jenny Shipley has developed a number of careers spanning different sectors from agriculture to politics to her own businesses in finance and energy. In each of these roles, she has demonstrated her immense power as a leader to collaborate and influence others to bring about sustainable change. She says of her time as Prime Minister that most of the policies enacted during her tenure were not revoked by the subsequent government. She was also the first woman to chair APEC (Asia-Pacific Economic Cooperation) in 1999. In the 13 years since she retired from politics, she has resumed her work in the private sector. She runs her own consultancy business and chairs a number of New Zealand companies. She was the Independent Chair of the Financial Services Council, and an independent director of a global Fortune 500 company. She was also the chair of Global Women NZ, the Vice President of the Club of Madrid, and a member of the World Women's Leaders Council.

Although Dame Jenny Shipley has worked across a number of sectors her focus and ambition has been driven by her strong commitment to leadership: "Leadership has always been a great interest of mine; shaping the future rather than describing the past has always intrigued me. I have always followed people who have done that."

It is evident her leadership focus has a strong commitment to enable more talent to develop in her organizations. She sees her role as a catalyst, someone who by virtue of her vision, capabilities, and networks can enact significant change: "My involvement is that ability to dare to think about the possibilities and be able to articulate what they might be. Then galvanize, work, and collaborate with others to make them happen." Despite this immense energy, Dame Jenny Shipley admits there is still a great deal to do to achieve success: "Leadership still keeps me up at night and gets me up in the morning: seeing things that need to be done. We need to galvanize, motivate, and enable people. I bring that to the chairmanship roles of companies I lead, in the talent, and also to the voluntary sector, where women are a huge and major part of what I do."

Building a leadership role that has the credibility to successfully demonstrate change with integrity and strong business acumen undoubtedly created the right conditions for Dame Jenny Shipley to be scouted for various board and other leadership positions. Her board positions traverse boundaries including Australia, Hong Kong, and China. Along with these opportunities, she has been able to create a platform that can be used to promote the broader diversity agenda for New Zealand and the Asia-Pacific region.

"To me, success is having a whole lot more people included. New Zealand is a very diverse economy, and I encourage them to participate so that it is a genuinely shared society that is safe for and respectful of difference. I am keen to condition those in dominant positions to understand why they will be benefit from diversity. There are social and economic benefits which will further contribute to an inclusive and cohesive society, to the benefit of us all. In the public and private sector, having a greater number of women in leadership is not only the proper and correct thing to do, it has social and economic benefit for New Zealand, creating a socially inclusive and cohesive society at home but also a relevant and effective society in the countries with whom we trade."

Her visibility and profile along with her commitment to innovative leadership means she is seen as a connector, someone who can help directors when they want to recruit onto nontraditional boards. Dame Jenny Shipley admits that despite the considerable progress of women on boards, evidenced in particular by the composition of the government, New Zealand still has a long way to go in the area of women on corporate boards. Rather than sitting on the sidelines, she has jumped in to create a solution and is part of the founding team that has established a number of initiatives with a clear focus on women in leadership: Global Women and Champions for Change.

Global Women provides training, coaching, and apprenticeship opportunities for board-potential women, and by leveraging her profile and relationship she has been able to build a collaborative model with corporates who nominate women for the program. "Champions for Change" was launched in 2015, working with C-Suite women and men who have committed to championing women into boards and C-Suite roles and to developing a far more diverse leadership in all aspects of New Zealand leadership areas of significance by 2020.

The interventions she has developed come from a place of really understanding the very personal challenges women face. She talks about the lack of confidence to the lack of accessible role models and champions for women, all of which she argues create barriers for women who want to move into leadership. She sees immense value in the network creating a strong, visible cohort of women who are ambitious for leadership but still need support to realize their ambitions: "For the majority of my leadership life, I had to hunt down people if I wanted their support." She attributes part of this to a natural reluctance amongst women to promote themselves: "It's not a natural thing for women to do, even though we overachieve, we are reluctant or unable to articulate our impact, not in an arrogant space but in an assured space. We must change this, for women in leadership roles can be a game-changing value proposition."

Dame Jenny Shipley describes how the Global Women's Network demonstrates the most impactful way women work together as leaders: "Women don't work in isolation, we work in an integrated setting, across business and economies: we all have to trade with the world so it just seems like a no brainer to have far more women involved, seeing that we all benefit from our collective success."

Dame Stephanie Shirley, Entrepreneur, UK

"I see myself as expressing my creativity not in the Arts but as an entrepreneur, in creating organizations," and this is what Dame Stephanie Shirley has achieved across many sectors. When she created her first organization in 1962 this was borne out of a need to build a female-friendly, unprejudiced organization. "I got a job in an IT company and had a team of engineers developing software for the ICT 1301 computer, which presented some interesting scientific issues. For 18 months I learned a great deal but came across the glass ceiling again and again. With lots of new management ideas and wanting to stretch into other areas but was told, 'this is nothing to do with you.'" That original company, Freelance Programmers, became F International (now part of the Sopra Group). It also had to be one which would allow her to care for her son who had been diagnosed with autism. To grow the business, she had to overcome a significant barrier; using her real name, Stephanie Shirley, she was unable to get appointments with potential clients. She took on the masculine form of her name, Steve, and got into clients' offices and from there on the business went from strength to strength.

The structure of the business initially provided jobs for women with children and this then developed to create career opportunities for women with dependents. At this point it grew to a 99 per cent female organization and the company was hit hard when the Equal Opportunities Act came in, requiring it to employ more men (creating another form of cultural shift in the organization!).

Steve Shirley's resilience can be traced back to her experiences as a child: she was a Kindertransport child who, along with her sister, came to the UK at the age of five, as unaccompanied refugees. Her experience of being placed with new parents, learning a new language, in a new environment, and adapting to everything new created a strong sense of purpose: "I learned that tomorrow is not like today, I learned about change. I swore to make mine a life worth saving, suffered from survivor guilt, somehow it all gets messed up and you feel you were partly to blame. I am a patriot and love the country that took me in and showed kindness, and this feeling is as strong today as it was 75 years ago."

Throughout her career, Steve Shirley has drawn upon a limited range of male models who have inspired her to be the leader she has become: "My first boss taught me the kind of boss I did not want to be. My foster father was very innovative and invented lots of things and that did have an influence. It gave me a wish to do new things. From my father I had inherited a love of learning. Other than that there were no role models. It was quite a lonely path."

When she was setting up the company, Steve Shirley describes how she did not have the networking resources to support her business development. As a result of these experiences she worked hard to create the support structures to enable more women to advance their careers: "The 'First Women's Group' was valuable: I was there as the leading IT woman." Over time, she has taken on other roles to support the development of women and for many years Steve Shirley mentored several female entrepreneurs. She continues to direct over many opportunities to other women. Of her support for women, Steve Shirley is clear about what she expects: "I coach people a lot of the time but have little patience for moaning. There is a cost of leadership."

Angelica Trigona, Chief Marketing Officer, Malta

Angelica Trigona has built a successful career in a male-dominated sector in a country where cultural norms still determine that women are primary carers for children. Her story is quite unique within this context, and demonstrates a conviction to improve gender diversity in her organizations and create a different model for her family.

Holding a degree in communications studies, Angelica has spent most of her career working in the IT sector, occupying various roles with an international software development and sales company. Her role there started with PR and Marketing, but as the company grew her role also increased: she developed the HR function while running the company's marketing activities and this eventually grew into a global role. As part of her HR role, she built relationships with mentors, providing critical feedback and coaching support for management team members.

One person she views as a mentor is a colleague she worked with closely; he was younger than her, and in him she identified a different style of working that helped her to develop an angle to her leadership approach that she describes as more balanced, calmer, and reflective.

Throughout her career there have been champions who recognized her potential and helped advance her career: "There have been CEOs who have valued my work ethic and were willing to recognize my work, which in turn helped advance my career. But I didn't have a formal mentor or coach to help me develop further via a structured program."

Working in HR provided a greater perspective on the challenges faced by women across the organization, and her seniority enabled her to do something about it. She reflects that she found it far easier to fight for the rights of others than for herself. When it came to female managers and prospective female managers, she tried to take on a championing role to support their leadership development: "I would make sure to groom female managers and pre-manager employers, to help them prepare answers, reports, or systems to help them get the necessary attention, results, and cooperation across the organization. At the beginning, I would often have to step in to help achieve things, to add weight due to my seniority, but I showed my female colleagues how they could address the challenge and communicate to get results." Her position is clear: her role is to promote talent with integrity, regardless of whether the person is a man or a women, but she also argues that women are still at a disadvantage: "The cliché is true – you do have to work twice as hard to get heard or get recognition for your work." As a result, her departments had higher retention rates of both female and male staff.

As her career flourished, Angelica had a son. During his first year her mother had helped with childcare. However, after her mother passed away the family had to make alternative choices. Her husband, who is self-employed, became the primary carer for their son, and Angelica pursued her career to very mixed reactions: "This was very unusual. It was different and it did create quite a few questions from family and friends. My son was serene and happy and so it worked. I have colleagues who have said they admire me – I am not being overly humble, but it's about taking a decision to live your life and making it work. You just try to see what situation you are in and what you need to do."

Angelica is aware she has an exceptional family set-up and is proud of the choice they have made, but she is clear about how she presents their life to her son: "With my son, I don't ram feminism down his throat, but I am careful to make sure the conversations we have present the right values and show parity between males and females. I'd love this to become a non-issue and, alongside education, live examples must be one of the ways to get there."

Joan H. Underwood, Regional Project Manager, Caribbean Leadership Project

Joan represents diversity as strength in every sense of the word. Her career has spanned public and political appointments across the Caribbean and Latin America. Joan's childhood was far from privileged. Her grandmother, who supported Joan and her four siblings through school, made sure the children had the chance to attend the best schools in Antigua. This formidable woman set up her own business, importing fruit and vegetables, when she first migrated to Antigua with a daughter and no husband for support. The stall took on special significance for the grandchildren: "We had to understand where we came from and the sacrifices made for us to go to the best schools. We had to work on the stall and understand the value of hard work. My grandmother did not have a formal education, but she was the smartest woman I have ever met and kept us grounded."

Joan's career started as a technical assistant in lab medicine but, frustrated by the lack of resources available, she wanted to make a difference at managerial level and returned to university where she obtained a masters in health services administration. On completion she became the first woman to manage the country's sole community hospital. The Chairman of the Board, Calvin Rodgers, invested in her development and championed her for the appointment: "He saw in me potential I did not see in myself. In my desire to live up to his expectation, it forced me to push past boundaries I would have put upon myself."

From this appointment she was involved in the setting-up of a drug rehab center established by Eric Clapton. Although these experiences were invaluable, Joan recognized she was at risk of creating a limiting career. To counter this, Joan returned to university again, this time to obtain an MBA. After her degree she became involved in lobbying for the rights of women and children, and was one of the founding members of POWA (Professional Organization for Women in Antigua/Barbuda).

Joan had continued the relationship with her champion, Calvin Rodgers, and during this period Joan realized the value of champions, who not only promoted her but also committed to what she believed in and willingly stood by her. Mr. Rodgers agreed to become a benefactor for POWA: "Talk about risk! We weren't very popular with the ruling party at the time. Among the issues we took up was a petition to raise the legal age of sexual consent. We were targets of attacks, personal attacks, vitriolic attacks against us, sexual orientation ... everything was fair game to discredit us. Having prominent men in the society standing up and saying they supported us, believed us ... and supporting the organization with their reputation and money, well this made it OK for others to support us."

The lobbying activities raised Joan's profile and in 2004, with the change in government administration, Joan was invited to join the diplomatic service as a non-resident ambassador for a number of Latin American countries. The invitation came from Prime Minister Baldwin Spencer, who went on to become another of her champions: "Given his background as a trade unionist, Prime Minister Spencer wanted someone with a strong focus not just on trade but also human development." This was not a full-time role and so Joan continued to work in the private sector, albeit with a great deal of flexibility to travel to assigned countries to conduct trade missions: "It proved to be such an enormous learning opportunity and gave me the opportunity to serve my country. It was one of the most fulfilling periods of my career."

During this period, Joan had also pursued studies in Human Resources and clearly saw the benefits of this discipline to her leadership: "That helped me to bring an even deeper level of understanding of human development and the various needs we have professionally and personally." It also provided the platform for her next role, once again championed by the Prime Minister, to lead on a process of public sector transformation. When this opportunity emerged, Joan had to consider taking a pay cut, moving from a lucrative private sector role to a public sector role. Her family and friends thought she had lost her mind, not least because the public sector role was not a permanent position. While on staff in the Office of the Prime Minister, Joan was assigned responsibility for the establishment and management of the Energy Desk and the creation of a national energy policy.

When the opportunity to join the Caribbean Leadership Program emerged, the Prime Minister was "unequivocal about his support and recognized that it presented an opportunity for Joan – and by extension, Antigua and Barbuda – to make a contribution at a regional level." Joan describes how the Prime Minister championed her: "He saw the potential, and without that I would have done well and made a contribution, but with him and because of him I have made a difference to a whole country."

The legacy of the champions on Joan has been to create a blueprint for the way she champions others; she recognizes the need to "stretch people": "It doesn't make sense to do the same thing every day. So, along with my direct reports, we talk about it, what it would feel like to take on new challenges; I won't tell you what to do but I am there to bounce ideas, and I will redirect you with questions. I'm not altruistic – the better they are, the less I have to do. I have to work smart, this means getting the right people to work." Joan is now very clear about her role as a champion: "My primary goal is not for you to like me, although that would be wonderful. Rather my desire is that when I leave, you feel you have learnt something and you have grown as a result of my having managed you." What gives her the sense of value and commitment to something bigger? She sums it up in a challenge issued to her by Dame Eugenia Charles, former Prime Minister of Dominica; "To those whom much is given, much is expected: making life better for others."

Appendix 1

TABLE 1 List of Commonwealth countries

Africa	Zambia	**North America**	Canada	**Caribbean**	Trinidad and Tobago
Africa	Uganda	**Pacific**	Australia	**Caribbean**	Jamaica
Africa	Botswana	**Pacific**	New Zealand	**Caribbean**	Barbados
Africa	Ghana	**Pacific**	Samoa	**Caribbean**	The Bahamas
Africa	Kenya	**Pacific**	Solomon Islands	**Caribbean**	Guyana
Africa	South Africa	**Pacific**	Tonga	**Caribbean**	St Vincent and the Grenadines
Africa	Malawi	**Pacific**	Tuvalu	**Caribbean**	Belize
Africa	Tanzania	**Pacific**	Vanuatu	**Caribbean**	Antigua and Barbuda
Africa	Namibia	**Pacific**	Fiji	**Caribbean**	Dominica
Africa	Nigeria	**Pacific**	Kiribati	**Caribbean**	Grenada
Africa	Mauritius	**Pacific**	Nauru	**Caribbean**	St Kitts and Nevis
Africa	Mozambique	**Pacific**	Papua New Guinea	**Caribbean**	St Lucia
Africa	Cameroon	**Asia**	Singapore	**Europe**	United Kingdom
Africa	Lesotho	**Asia**	Malaysia	**Europe**	Cyprus
Africa	Rwanda	**Asia**	Maldives	**Europe**	Malta
Africa	Seychelles	**Asia**	India		
Africa	Sierra Leone	**Asia**	Bangladesh		
Africa	Swaziland	**Asia**	Sri Lanka		
		Asia	Pakistan		
		Asia	Brunei-Darussalam		

TABLE 2   Ranking of countries according to the World Economic Forum Global
Gender Gap Survey (2015)

1	Iceland	28	Luxembourg	55	Croatia	82	Uruguay
2	Finland	29	Spain	56	Ukraine	83	Albania
3	Norway	30	Cuba	57	Poland	84	El Salvador
4	Sweden	31	Argentina	58	Bolivia	85	Georgia
5	Denmark	32	Belarus	59	Singapore	86	Venezuela
6	Nicaragua	33	Barbados	60	Lao PDR	87	China
7	Rwanda	34	Malawi	61	Thailand	88	Uganda
8	Ireland	35	Bahamas	62	Estonia	89	Guatemala
9	Philippines	36	Austria	63	Zimbabwe	90	Slovak Republic
10	Belgium	37	Kenya	64	Guyana	91	Greece
11	Switzerland	38	Lesotho	65	Israel	92	Swaziland*
12	Germany	39	Portugal	66	Chile	93	Hungary
13	New Zealand	40	Namibia	67	Kyrgyz Republic	94	Azerbaijan
14	Netherlands	41	Madagascar	68	Bangladesh	95	Cyprus
15	Latvia	42	Mongolia	69	Italy	96	Czech Republic
16	France	43	Kazakhstan	70	Macedonia, FYR	97	Indonesia
17	Burundi	44	Lithuania	71	Brazil	98	Brunei Darussalam
18	South Africa	45	Peru	72	Romania	99	Malta
19	Canada	46	Panama	73	Honduras	100	Belize
20	United States	47	Tanzania	74	Montenegro	101	Ghana
21	Ecuador	48	Costa Rica	75	Russian Federation	102	Tajikistan
22	Bulgaria	49	Trinidad and Tobago	76	Vietnam	103	Armenia
23	Slovenia	50	Cape Verde	77	Senegal	104	Japan
24	Australia	51	Botswana	78	Dominican Republic	105	Maldives
25	Moldova	52	Jamaica	79	Sri Lanka	106	Mauritius
26	United Kingdom	53	Colombia	80	Mexico	107	Malaysia
27	Mozambique	54	Serbia	81	Paraguay	108	Cambodia

(continued)

TABLE 2   Continued

109	Suriname	118	Nigeria	127	Ethiopia	136	Cote d'Ivoire
110	Burkina Faso	119	Zambia	128	Oman	137	Iran, Islamic Rep.
111	Liberia*	120	Bhutan	129	Egypt	138	Mali
112	Nepal	121	Angola	130	Saudi Arabia	139	Syria
113	Kuwait	122	Fiji	131	Mauritania	140	Chad
114	India	123	Tunisia*	132	Guinea*	141	Pakistan
115	United Arab Emirates	124	Bahrain	133	Morocco	142	Yemen
116	Qatar	125	Turkey	134	Jordan		
117	Korea Rep.	126	Algeria	135	Lebanon		

Appendix 2: Gender at Work

A majority of people would say they "know" intuitively that there are significant gender differences, and would be happy to start listing them, but please beware of that kind of stereotyping knowledge … although intuition can be valuable in helping us know and decide about some areas in our lives and work, it is also prone to bias and error. If you doubt this, remember that women were believed to be less capable than men, less able to manage their own affairs, even in the so-called developed countries until very recently, in some cases renouncing, on marriage, their rights to manage their own property and taxes until past the middle of the 20th century. And all this in the face of overwhelming evidence of women operating effectively across a number of spheres, not just in the home, but in agriculture, in factories, in laboratories, in shops, and, in England, as a ruler. Rationality, evidence, and logic do not always trump belief!

So what can we derive from science – neuroscience in particular – that might help us better understand how men and women might think and behave differently, how might that affect how they behave at work, and what impact might any differences – not just confidence – contribute to their career progression?

Brain-based differences

It is indeed true that men and women are, *on average*, different as regards their brain structures. A meta-analysis by a team from Cambridge

University, published in February 2014, which looked at research covering all ages, from birth to 80, has confirmed that women's brains are, on the whole, smaller than men's (by between 8 and 13 per cent), which is not surprising as women are, on average, smaller than men. However, differences in volume and density were not evenly distributed, so that although the finding in this research was that men had both more grey and white matter overall, consistently with greater overall size, in some areas women had more or denser grey and white matter. But we do not yet know "what behavioural effects – if any – these differences might elicit."[1]

Other researchers have found that overall, women have denser grey matter than men, yet others that women have more grey matter and men more white, when adjusted for size. One study found a slight correlation between overall brain size and corpus callosum size and intelligence, but the majority have not.

If there is a consensus, it is that (structural) gender-based differences in human brains are "small, subtle, few and of unknown function."[2]

Neuronal structure is, however, very far from being the whole story when it comes to the brain. Male and female brains appear to differ in the *connections* between neurons that are shaped by experience as well as by genes, and in their *neurochemistry*.

We are only just beginning to understand just how complex the interactions are between structures, neuronal connections, and chemistry in the brain and between them and external experience. That brain plasticity, the capacity to change, extends throughout life is now well-known, with the implications for learning, development, and sustainable behavior change only just beginning to be explored.

We also know that neuroscience is a rapidly evolving discipline, and the non-invasive imaging tools and techniques that are available now are enabling more precise observations, revealing new insights, and sometimes correcting previous findings. For example, it has been said for many years that the corpus callosum – that broad, thick ribbon of connective neural fibers joining the two hemispheres of the brain that carries much of the communication between them – is larger in women's brains. That is now controversial, with more recent investigations indicating that it might only be thicker at one point, if at all, depending on how it is measured. Also, some studies show that when properly adjusted for overall volume, differences between the sexes become insignificant.[3]

There are also those who say that women's limbic systems are bigger, and that this might be the underpinning of women's superior emotional skills as the "limbic system" is a shorthand for those structures of the brain involved in emotional processing. But that is doubly an oversimplification, as firstly the brain's emotional processing is much more complex and engages more elements than any one system implies, and secondly, although it may indeed be the case that some structures involved in emotional processing are proportionately bigger in women (for example, the anterior cingulate gyrus), others, such as the amygdala, are bigger in men.

Oh and did I mention that these findings tend to relate to the average female or male? That there are those women whose brains are much bigger than some men's? You get the picture. Yes there are differences, but we don't yet have an accurate, agreed map of them, and most importantly, we don't know what they mean in terms of behavior and performance. There is one theory that has been gaining traction since 2004,[4] that at least some of the structural gender differences in the brain are intended to be compensatory for other differences, such as hormonal changes related to reproduction, their purpose being to drive more similar behaviors.

Diane Halpern, in her book, *Sex Differences in Cognitive Abilities*,[5] puts it well: "Size cannot be considered without reference to all the other systems and structures which reflect brain activity. Single dimensions cannot be used in understanding systems in which multiple components interact." She could have added structure to size.

So if women and men are much more similar than different in the brains, why are we looking at the neuroscience of behavior? First of all, because even small differences in the brain can mean differences in behaviors and the way each gender experiences the world. Secondly, to debunk some of the mythology about what women can or cannot do, due to their neuro-biology, and thirdly, to examine under that lens too what it may be that championship contributes to women's success.

Connections

In 2013, an important study from the University of Pennsylvania by Ragini Verma et al.,[6] showed that, in addition to structural differences, there are significant and consistent differences in the connective path-ways in adult male and female brains (the connectome). Essentially, the research showed that women's brains had more connections *across* the hemispheres and men's *along* them, and that this was reversed in the connections for the cerebellum, where men had more connec-tions between the hemispheres of the cerebellum. Interestingly, these differences were significant from age 13 onwards.

Even taking into account challenges to this research that showed the differ-ences might be less significant than stated, it seems that this wiring pattern might be interpreted as underpinning some observed behavioral differences, such as women's ability to access resources across both hemispheres more efficiently (which for some indicates a better ability to interact socially, and is also sometimes seen as an ability to use both analytical and intuitive thinking) and men's ability to link perception to action more effectively.

The implication that these differences are somehow "hard wired" is misleading. Just as is the implication that, if they are not hard wired, they are due primarily to cultural influences.

It is possible, if not more likely, that a combination of genetic expression triggered by the onslaught of the sex hormones that stimulate physical as well as mental changes in puberty to prepare for reproduction and adulthood in brain and body, shapes brain connections differently along gender lines, as well as individual experience (for which both culture and nurture are factors).

The difference in how male and female brains might mobilize their different structures, reflected in the average patterns of the connectome, regardless of its causation, may underlie different habitual cognitive and emotional processes or pathways, that is, ways of experiencing, thinking, of solving problems, and even attitudes. So, for example, some maintain that the amygdala reacts differently in men and women. The amygdala is that part of the brain that appears to be crucial in the process of assigning meaning to incoming stimuli from all the senses. That meaning is defined by the emotions, in a spectrum from good–approach to bad–avoid. Some studies have found that women tend to focus more on the negative than positive meaning stimuli. That has been linked with women's greater tendency to focus on critical rather than positive comments and feedback.

Chemistry

Men and women also differ in the chemicals that affect the brain, the hormones and neurotransmitters, and their receptors.[7]

For example, it has been known for some time that women and men do not suffer equally from some psychiatric conditions associated with serotonin, such as depression, anxiety, and suicide.[8] Women have higher rates of depression and more women suffer from anxiety, whereas more men, especially young men, commit suicide.[9] A study from the Swedish Karolinska Institute showed that women have a greater number of the most common serotonin receptors than men and lower levels of the protein that transports serotonin back into the nerve cells that secrete it.[10]

Yet others have found gender-based differences in dopamine receptor levels, which could also be reflected in differences in dopamine-related disorders,[11] and differences have been also been found in how oxytocin and vasopressin affect men and women.[12] We know that serotonin, dopamine, and oxytocin play roles in states such as pleasure, anxiety, optimism, and trust that are related to confidence, that in turn is one of the personality characteristics, together with a lack of neuroticism, associated with leaders.

As we said earlier, the genome is like a plan that is subject to influence and change. So even though there may be a genetic predisposition to anxiety, other factors, such as stress, might exacerbate the anxiety and yet others, such as high quality nurturing in infancy and early childhood, may play a role in developing the capacity to dampen the effects of stress and even in reducing the impact of lower serotonin levels through other as yet unexplained mechanisms.

So although it may indeed be the case that women can be, on average, more anxious than men about their performance in the workplace, and that this could be one factor in the often observed behavior of perfectionism, there are a number of different factors at play and it would be dangerous to assume this automatically of all women.

Perhaps the best known "neurochemical differentiator" between genders is testosterone. It is testosterone, known as the male hormone, that creates the conditions for the main male physical characteristics, firstly in the womb and then at puberty. Although both men and women secrete testosterone, men on average have about eight to ten times more than women. A higher level of testosterone is correlated with a range of typically male behaviours, including aggression, risk tolerance, and focus. Social status and dominance in primates is positively correlated to testosterone levels, when the position is not under threat.

Testosterone is also correlated with social challenge.[13] An animal that has recently won a fight (either male or female) is statistically more likely to win the next fight due to testosterone-induced increases in the oxygen-carrying capacity of hemoglobin and appetite for risk. Winning keeps raising testosterone levels until there are too many high-risk battles and the animal is weakened and dominance is lost.[14]

Notes and References

Introduction

1. Especially her book, Hewitt, A. A. (2013) *(Forget a Member) Find a Sponsor: The New Way to Fast-Track Your Career* (Boston, MA: Harvard Business Review Press).
2. Financial Times Top 100 listed companies (UK).
3. Standard & Poor's Top 500 companies (US).
4. Sheryl Sandberg, from CNN. Opinion on the News, by Sheryl Sandberg, Special to CNN. 18 March 2013.
5. Maya is a fictitious amalgamation of many of our respondents.

1   The CHAMP Model

1. http://fortune.com/fortune500/.
2. https://www.imf.org/external/np/speeches/2014/091214.htm.
3. Catalyst – http://www.catalyst.org/legislative-board-diversity.
4. Listed companies (NEDs and EDs).
5. Interview with Alex Johnston, Executive Director, Catalyst Canada.
6. Terminology used by Stephen Sidebottom, Standard Chartered Bank.
7. W. F. Cascio (2006) *Managing Human Resources: Productivity, Quality of Work Life, Profits*, 7th ed. (Burr Ridge, IL: Irwin/McGraw-Hill) and T. R. Mitchell, B. C. Holtom and T. W. Lee (2001) "How to keep your best employees: Developing an effective retention policy," *Academy of Management Executive*, 15, pp. 96–108.
8. Illustration from R. Sherwin (2014) "Why Women Are More Effective Leaders Than Men," *Business Insider*, 24 January.
9. T. S. Mohr (2014) "Why women don't apply for jobs unless they're 100% qualified," *Harvard Business Review*, 25 August, https://hbr.org/2014/08/why-women-dont-apply-for-jobs-unless-theyre-100-qualified/.

10. Sheryl Sandberg (2013) *Lean In: Women, Work and the Will to Lead* (New York: Alfred A. Knopf, Random House).
11. Speaker, BNY Mellon Womenomics Conference, 8 April 2015, http://women omics.co.uk.
12. Victor Oladapo (2014) "The impact of talent management on retention," *Journal of Business Studies Quarterly*, 5(3).
13. http://www.weforum.org/women-leaders-and-gender-parity.
14. M. J. Silverstein and K. Sayre (2009) "The female economy," *Harvard Business Review*, September, https://hbr.org/2009/09/the-female-economy.
15. "On the rise and online, female consumers in Asia," Economist Intelligence Unit Report, 16 December 2014, http://www.economistinsights.com/marketing-consumer/analysis/rise-and-online.

2   Women in Leadership – What's Going On?

1. Global Gender Gap Report (2014) World Economic Forum http://reports.weforum.org/global-gender-gap-report-2014/ (accessed 4/3/15).
2. Appendix 1: Table 1 contains a full list of current Commonwealth countries.
3. Data drawn from "Shifting Gears in Women's Leadership" report prepared by Dr Shaheena Janjuha Jivraj for the Commonwealth Secretariat. Presented at the Women in Leadership forum, Kenya, June 2015; Commonwealth Secretariat, UN Women and the International Labour Organisation (ILO). Data collected between September 2014 and January 2015.
4. ibid.
5. ibid.
6. ibid.
7. Countries included have at least ten listed companies on the stock market.
8. Data drawn from "Shifting Gears in Women's Leadership."
9. ibid. State-owned enterprises refer to government corporations and parastatals (100 per cent government owned).
10. State-owned enterprises refer to government corporations and parastatals (100 per cent government owned).
11. S. Nadkarni and E. Oon (2015) "The Rise of Women in Society: Enablers and Inhibitors, a Global Study," initial findings released at Womenomics Conference, London, 8 April 2015.

3   Barriers to Progress: Confidence and Bias

1. The Institute of Leadership and Management, in the UK, conducted a study in 2011, simply asking British women, in a series of questions, how confident

they felt in their professions. Not very, as it turns out. Half of the women reported feelings of self-doubt about their performance and careers, while less than a third of male respondents reported self-doubt. Linda Babcock, a professor of economics at Carnegie Mellon University, and the author of *Women Don't Ask*, has uncovered a similar lack of confidence among American women, with concrete consequences.

2. Linda Babcock, *Women Don't Ask*, cited in K. Kay and C. Shipman (2014) *The Confidence Code: The Science and Art of Self-Assurance—What Women Should Know* (London: HarperCollins) Kindle edition, pp. 13–14.

3. Kay and Shipman (2014) *The Confidence Code*.

4. E. Westly (2012) "Different shades of blue, his brain her brain," *Scientific American Mind*, special edition, Summer, p. 34.

5. M. Konner (2015) *Women After All: Sex, Evolution and the End of Male Supremacy* (New York: W. W. Norton & Company).

6. M. Johnson and V. S. Helgeson (2002) "Sex Differences in Response to Evaluative Feedback: A Field Study," American Psychological Association; Kay and Shipman (2014) *The Confidence Code*.

7. L. Eliot (2012) "The truth about boys and girls: his brain her brain," *Scientific American Mind,* special edition, Summer, p. 34

8. Put forward by Albert Bandura in 1977, and later expanded by others.

9. K. Kay and C. Shipman (2014) *The Confidence Code*, p. 12.

10. Apparently men too suffer from that feeling, but tend to be better able to ignore that voice.

11. P. R. Clance (1985) *The Impostor Phenomenon: Overcoming the Fear That Haunts Your Success* (Atlanta: Peachtree).

12. Kay and Shipman (2014) *The Confidence Code*, Chapter 3, "Wired for Confidence," passim.

13. T. Swart, K. Chisholm, and P. Brown (2015) *Neuroscience for Leadership: The Brain Gain Advantage* (London: Palgrave Macmillan), p. 58 and Chapter 3, "The New Model Leader."

14. Swart, Chisholm, and Brown (2015) *Neuroscience for Leadership*. Cinderella syndrome is also known as the tiara syndrome.

15. When we discuss luck in this context we are referring to actions relating to chance, outcomes as a result of unplanned activities, not fate, nor a sense of something deeper or mystical.

16. Often attributed to Samuel Goldwyn.

17. A pattern of behaviour that had become an automated habit over time.

18. Interview with Stephen Sidebottom, Standard Chartered Bank, February 2015.

19. See, for example, D. Kahneman (2011) *Thinking, Fast and Slow* (London: Allen Lane, Penguin), or Swart, Chisholm, and Brown (2015) *Neuroscience for Leadership*.

20. G. Stulp, A. Buunk, S. Verhulst, and T. V. Pollet (2012) "Tall claims? Sense and nonsense about the importance of height of US presidents," *The Leadership Quarterly*, http://dx.doi.org/10.1016/j.leaqua.2012.09.002.

21. Catalyst Research (2007) "The Double-Bind Dilemma for Women in Leadership: Damned if You Do, Doomed if You Don't."

22. Sheryl Sandberg (2013) *Lean In: Women, Work and the Will to Lead* (New York: Alfred A. Knopf, Random House), p. 41.

23. Do try to watch it if you can still access it on YouTube: https://www.youtube.com/watch?v=B8gz-jxjCmg.

24. Kathleen Davis (2014) "The one word men never see in their performance reviews," *Fast Company*, 27 August 27, accessed 31 December 2014.

25. Quoted by Jessica Nordell in an article in *New Republic* on 28 August 2014.

26. Although one of our interviewees, a male to female transgender working in the Museum sector, said she did not experience any less respect as a woman, saying that her own organization had been fairly free of gender bias.

27. S. J. Leslie, A. Cimpian, M. Meyer, and E. Freeland (2015) "Expectations of brilliance underlie gender distributions across academic disciplines," *Science*, 347 (6219), pp. 262–5.

28. See, for example, S. J. Ceci, D. K. Ginther, S. Khan, and W. M. Williams (2015) "Women in Science, the Path to Progress," *Scientific American Mind*, January/February.

29. See also Konner (2015) *Women After All*.

30. Bandura, for example, also maintained that people could learn by watching others, not just from their own experiences and the feedback they got from their own actions.

31. S. Harter (2012) *The Construction of the Self: Developmental and Sociocultural Foundations* (New York: Guilford Press).

32. L. Eliot (2012) "The truth about boys and girls," p. 34.

33. https://www.youtube.com/watch?v=Ks-_Mh1QhMc&list=PLheH9TdTMp9yDxZivmwDnkQ329DzijtDE.

4   Why Championing Works So Well for Women

1. Story repeated in K. Kay and C. Shipman (2014) *The Confidence Code: The Science and Art of Self-Assurance—What Women Should Know* (New York: HarperBusiness), Kindle edition, p. 120.

2. Amy J. C. Cuddy, Caroline A. Wilmuth, and Dana R. Carney (2012) "The Benefit of Power Posing Before a High-Stakes Social Evaluation," Harvard Business School Working Paper, No. 13-027, September. Accessed 22 June 2015, http://nrs.harvard.edu/urn-3:HUL.InstRepos:9547823.

3. E. Ranehill, A. Dreber, M. Johannesson, S. Leiberg, S. Sul, and R. A. Weber (2015) "Assessing the robustness of power posing: No effect on hormones and risk tolerance in a large sample of men and women," *Psychological Science*, March.
4. See Marshall Goldsmith, "Try Feedforward Instead of Feedback," Leader to Leader Institute, www.mashallgoldsmithlibrary.com.
5. "Shifting Gears in Women's Leadership," report prepared by Dr Shaheena Janjuha Jivraj for the Commonwealth Secretariat. Presented at the Women in Leadership forum, Kenya, June 2015; Commonwealth Secretariat, UN Women and the International Labour Organisation (ILO). Data collected between September 2014 and January 2015.
6. B. Judge (2015) "We need female chief executives not just non-executives," *Financial Times*, 29 April.

5   Getting Ready for Championship

1. Cited in Kathleen Davis (2014) "The one word men never see in their performance reviews" *Fast Company*, 27 August, accessed 31 December 2014.
2. T. Swart, K. Chisholm, and P. Brown (2015) *Neuroscience for Leadership: Harnessing the Brain Gain Advantage* (London: Palgrave MacMillan), pp. 9–13. The attachment emotions are love/trust and joy/excitement; escape/avoidance/survival emotions are fear, anger, disgust, shame, and sadness. Surprise/startle is a potentiator that facilitates change in emotional states.
3. R. Epstein (2000) *The Big Book of Creativity Games* (London: McGraw Hill).
4. A. Einstein (1979) *Albert Einstein: The Human Side: Glimpses from his Archives* (Princeton: Princeton University Press).
5. D. Kahneman (2011) *Thinking, Fast and Slow* (London: Allen Lane, Penguin), p. 41.
6. R. Baumeister and J. Tierney (2011) *Willpower: Rediscovering the Greatest Human Strength* (London: Penguin).
7. Bandura in Baumeister and Tierney (2011), p. 69.
8. Or indeed for those women who return but leave again within a very short period of time – less than six months.

6   Developing the Championing Relationship

1. C. D. Frith (2007) *Making Up The Mind: How the Brain Creates our Mental World* (Oxford: Wiley-Blackwell).
2. M. Angier and B. Axelrod (2014) "Realizing the power of talented women," *McKinsey Quarterly*, September.

3. T. Swart, K. Chisholm, and P. Brown (2015) *Neuroscience for Leadership: Harnessing the Brain Gain Advantage* (London: Palgrave Macmillan).
4. Heidi Grant Halvorson (2015) "How the shape of your face affects the way you're perceived at work," *Fast Company* blog, accessed 7 April 2015.
5. Nancy Kline's *Time to Think* (London: Octopus Books, 1999) is the classic on this subject and very worth reading.
6. Simons and Chabris, 1999: https://www.youtube.com/watch?v=vJG698U2Mvo.

7   Creating a Brand Worth Championing

1. D. Ulrich and N. Smallwood (2007) "Building a leadership brand," *Harvard Business Review*, July-August.
2. T. Peters (1997) "The brand called you," *Fast Company*, http://www.fastcompany.com/28905/brand-called-you.
3. http://www.statista.com/statistics/278414/number-of-worldwide-social-network-users/.
4. *Oxford English Dictionary*: http://www.oxforddictionaries.com/definition/english/old-boy-network.
5. Quoted in K. Kay and C. Shipman (2014) *The Confidence Code: The Science and Art of Self-Assurance—What Women Should Know* (New York: HarperBusiness), Kindle edition, pp. 151–2.
6. A. H. Eagly and B. T. Johnson (1990) "Gender and Leadership Styles: A Meta-Analysis," University of Connecticut, DigitalCommons@UConn, CHIP Documents (Center for Health, Intervention, and Prevention).
7. A. H. Eagly and L. Carli (2003) "The female leadership advantage: An evaluation of the evidence," *The Leadership Quarterly*, 14, pp. 807–34. Referenced in D. F. Halpern and F. M. Cheung (2008) *Women at the Top: Powerful Leaders Tell Us How to Combine Work and Family* (Oxford: Wiley-Blackwell).
8. M. S. Granovetter (1973) "The strength of weak ties," *American Journal of Sociology*, 78 (6), pp. 1360–80.
9. D. Carnegie (2006) *How to Win Friends and Influence People* (London: Vermilion).
10. M. Gladwell (2000) *The Tipping Point: How Little Things Can Make a Big Difference* (London: Abacus).
11. http://www.brandwatch.com/2015/01/men-vs-women-active-social-media/.
12. Z. King and A. Scott (2014) *Who's in Your Personal Boardroom? How to Choose People, Assign Roles and Have Conversations with Purpose* (CreateSpace Independent Publishing Platform).

8   The Power of Championing: Unleashing the Power of Female Leaders

1. Extracts from "The Economic Power of Women's Empowerment," keynote speech by Christine Lagarde, Managing Director, International Monetary Fund, Tokyo, 12 September 2014.
2. Posted by Moises Naim: "The Lagarde consensus," online article in *The Atlantic*, 12 April 2015. http://www.theatlantic.com/international/archive/2015/04/the-christine-lagarde-consensus-imf/390309/.
3. Dame Stephanie Shirley (2012) LET IT GO (Andrews UK).
4. D. Goleman (2000) *Harvard Business Review*, March-April.
5. In T. Swart, K. Chisholm, and P. Brown (2015) *Neuroscience for Leadership: The Brain Gain Advantage* (London: Palgrave Macmillan).
6. It would appear that where the outcome is dependent on the individual's own perception of competence or likelihood of success, men's higher levels of confidence and greater propensity towards over-optimism is a critical factor: "Due to lower confidence in their knowledge and information, women perceive more 'uncertainty about uncertainty' than men." (R. Schubert, M. Gysler, M. Brown, and H-W Brachinger (2000) "Gender specific attitudes towards risk and ambiguity: An experimental investigation," paper, July, Centre For Economic Research, Swiss Federal Institute of Technology, Zurich). See also S. T. Trautmann, F. M. Vielder, and P. P. Wakker (2008) "Causes of ambiguity aversion: Known versus unknown preferences," *Journal of Risk and Uncertainty*, 36, pp. 225–43; A. Wieland and R. Sarin (2012) "Gender differences in risk aversion: A theory of when and why," working paper, UCLA Anderson School of Management; L. Borghans, B. H. H. Golsteyn, J. J. Heckman, and H. Meijers (2009) "Gender differences in risk aversion and ambiguity aversion," IZA discussion papers no. 3985; A. Dreber and M. Hoffman (2010) "Biological basis of sex differences in risk aversion and competitiveness," paper, UCLA.
7. S. R. Fisk (2014) "Risky Spaces, Gendered Places: The Effect of Risky Settings on Women's and Men's Negative Affect and Task Performance," paper presented on 18 August 2014 in San Francisco at the American Sociological Association's 109th Annual Meeting.
8. *Harvard Business Review* article online on 15 March 2012: "Are Women Better Leaders than Men?"
9. 360° evaluations are multi-source feedback tools that garner assessments against competencies from those close to the person evaluated, but from different levels: peers, direct reports, line managers, senior managers, and those they do business with without a direct reporting line in either direction.

They have some weaknesses that undermine their claim to accuracy, but used appropriately can be very useful tools for evaluating strengths and weaknesses in leaders and managers, as perceived by those who work with them.

9   Case Studies

1. Mervyn Davies went on to become the Chairman of Standard Chartered Bank and was ennobled as Lord Davies of Abersoch. He authored the influential Davies report in the UK, advocating for more women on boards in 2011.

Appendixes

1. A. N. V. Ruigrok, G. Salimi-Khorshidi, M-Ch Lai, S. Baron-Cohen, M. V. Lombardo, R. J. Tait, and J. Suckling (2014) "A meta-analysis of sex differences in human brain structure," *Neuroscience & Biobehavioral Reviews*, Volume 39, February, pp. 34–50.
2. M. F. Bear, B. W. Connors, and M. A. Paradiso (2007) *Neuroscience: Exploring the Brain*, 3rd ed. (Philadelphia: Lippincott, Williams & Wilkins), Chapter 7.
3. K. M. Bishop and D. Wahlsten (1997) "Sex differences in the human corpus callosum: myth or reality?", *Neuroscience & Biobehavioral Reviews*, 21(5), 581–601. http://www.dana.org/Cerebrum/2014/Equal_%E2%89%A0_The_ Same_Sex_Differences_in_the_Human_Brain/#sthash.09xtQtTz.dpuf.
4. Gert de Vries (2004) "Minireview: Sex differences in adult and developing brains: compensation, compensation, compensation," *Endocrinology*, 145 (3), published online 2013.
5. D. Halpern (2013) *Sex Differences in Cognitive Abilities*, 4th ed. (Hove: Psychology Press).
6. M. Ingalhalikar, A. Smith, D. Parker, T. D. Satterthwaite, M. A. Elliott, K. Ruparel, H. Hakonarson, R. E. Gur, R. C. Gur, and R. Verma (2013) "Sex differences in the structural connectome of the human brain," *Proceedings of the National Academy of Sciences of the United States of America*, 111 (2), pp. 823–8.
7. The main hormones are: cortisol, adrenalin, testosterone, estrogen/progesterone. The main neurotransmitters are: dopamine, serotonin, oxytocin and noradrenalin.
8. Elizabeth H. Gorman (2006) "Work uncertainty and the promotion of professional women: The case of law firm partnership," *Social Forces*, 85(2), pp. 865–90.

9. P. M. Lewinsohn, T. E. Joiner Jr, and P. Rohde (2001) "Evaluation of cognitive diathesis-stress models in predicting major depressive disorder in adolescents," *Journal of Abnormal Psychology*, 110, pp. 203–15.

10. It is this protein that the most common antidepressants (SSRIs) block. H. Jovanovic, J. Lundberg, P. Karlsson, A. Cerin, T. Saijo, A. Varrone, C. Halldin, and A. L. Nordström (2008) "Sex differences in the serotonin 1A receptor and serotonin transporter binding in the human brain measured by PET," *Neuroimage*, 39(3) pp. 1408–19.

11. A number of studies (on monkeys and humans) have shown that those individuals, both male and female, with a particular version of the gene that encodes the protein, 5 HTT (that removes serotonin released into the synapse) are more prone to anxiety and depression. See V. Kaasinen, K. Någren, J. Hietala, L. Farde, and J. O. Rinne (2001) "Sex differences in Extrastriatal Dopamine D2-like receptors in the human brain," *American Journal of Psychiatry*, 158(2), pp. 308–11.

12. S. K. Lynn, E. A. Hoge, L. E. Fischer, L. F. Barrett, and N. M. Simon (2014) "Gender differences in oxytocin-associated disruption of decision bias during emotion perception," *Psychiatry Research*, 219 (1), pp. 198–203; J. K. Rilling, A. C. Demarco, P. D. Hackett, X. Chen, P. Gautam, S. Stair, E. Haroon, R. Thompson, B. Ditzen, R. Patel, and G. Pagnoni (2014) "Sex differences in the neural and behavioral response to intranasal oxytocin and vasopressin during human social interaction," *Psychoneuroendocrinology*, 39, pp. 237–48.

13. C. Eisenegger, J. Haushofer, and E. Fehr (2011) "The role of testosterone in social interaction," *Trends in Cognitive Sciences*, 15(6), pp. 263–71.

14. T. Swart, K. Chisholm, and P. Brown (2015) *Neuroscience for Leadership: The Brain Gain Advantage* (London: Palgrave Macmillan), Chapter 4, p. 63.

Index

References to figures are shown in *italics*. References to tables are shown in **bold**. References to notes consist of the page number with, in brackets, the number of the chapter followed by the letter "n" followed by the number of the note, e.g. 218 (6n5) refers to note 5 under Chapter 6 on page 218.

Printed and bound by CPI Group (UK) Ltd, Croydon, CR0 4YY